What the reviewers said . . .

In this fine, through-the-... ...evolutionary China, such heroes as Dr. Norman Bethune, Mao Tse-tung, and Chou En-lai sweat and fuss like the rest of humanity."
— Brendan Hawley, Ottawa *Citizen*

"A robust and appealing character. . . . Straightforward and blunt, and not given overmuch to introspection."
— Margaret MacMillan, *The Toronto Sunday Star*

"*China Nurse* is a book of bizarre contrasts: One day, (the author) is fighting the squalor of women giving birth to children already dead from dirt; and, the next, she is attending a Christian wedding in the same village, complete with glowing bride in exquisitely embroidered red silk and fabulous presents. . . . A book on the strength of the human spirit and an insight, more valuable than many a political history, into the death of one society and the birth of a new one."
— Dan Kislenko, Hamilton *Spectator*

"A remarkable woman, she comes across as a strong character able to tolerate the foulest conditions and not lose her sense of humor."
— Penny Edwards, Montreal *Gazette*

"With Norman Bethune during part of her work-travel sojourn, Ewen healed the sick, bandaged the wounded, and took verbal (usually sexist) abuse from the overrated doctor."
— Anthony Chan, *Quill & Quire*

CANADIAN NURSE IN CHINA

JEAN EWEN

Goodread Biographies

To my own *hsiao kuies* (little devils), Isobel, Terry, Jody, and Seana.

CANADIAN CATALOGUING IN PUBLICATION DATA

Ewen, Jean.
  Canadian nurse in China

Previously published as: China nurse 1932-1939.
Toronto: McClelland and Stewart, 1981.
ISBN 0-88780-105-6

1. Ewen, Jean.   2. Missionaries, Medical – China –
Biography.   3. Nurses – China – Biography.
4. Sino-Japanese Conflict, 1937-1945 – Personal
narratives, Canadian.   I. Title.   II. Title: China
nurse 1932-1939.

R722.32.E93A3 1983   610.69′5   C83-098338-4

Published in hardcover as *China Nurse 1932-1939*

First published in 1981 by McClelland and Stewart
  Limited

Published in paperback 1983 by
  Goodread Biographies
Canadian Lives series publisher: James Lorimer

Goodread Biographies is the paperback imprint of
Formac Publishing Company Limited
333 - 1657 Barrington Street
Halifax, Nova Scotia
B3J 2A1

Printed and bound in Canada

Acknowledgements

I would like to thank Terrence McCartney Filgate, Nigel
Booth, and Kim Abbot, for their encouragement;
Pierre Berton, who felt that the book had merit; and my
children, Laura, Tom, and Mike, who supported me.

FOREWORD

The events in these pages are long past–I do not attempt to judge whether they are right or wrong. No innuendo is intended, although I am sure there are those who will shout liar, prevaricator, Trotskyite, or whatever. Should you wish to verify the events, be my guest. An enterprising individual with a knack for diligent search will find them to be true. Life before and during those far-off thirties was sometimes stormy, sometimes frustrating, but it was never dull.

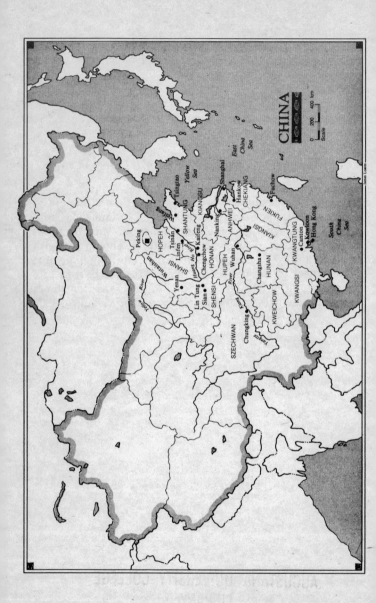

CHINA

Scale
0 200 400 km

CHAPTER ONE

I do not remember my thoughts as the great *White Empress* eased away from the Granville Street pier in Vancouver in March 1933. I do, however, recall that as a dockside band played "Will Ye No Come Back Again," a great loneliness overwhelmed me. I looked at my two friends, Rose Martin and Agnes Shaeffer. Both had tears in their eyes.

"Stop blubbering," I said, reminding them that we had got what we wanted. We were on our way to China, and it was too late now to change our minds.

The Canada we were leaving behind was locked in the Depression, and as recently graduated nurses, we were lucky to have a job of any sort, let alone one that promised such great adventure. When Agnes had first suggested that we apply for the jobs, Rose and I had gone along with her for a lark. Nurses were a dime a dozen in those days, and we never seriously considered that we might be chosen. But we soon found ourselves caught up in interviews and applications to the Franciscan Fathers of the Sacred Heart Province. Then one day we learned that we would soon be off as missionaries to China, of all places.

Before leaving for the East, I wanted to visit my family in Toronto. It was not a happy visit. My father was one of eight Communists who had been arrested for sedition. My visit coincided with his appeal hearings.

My father and I had never been close. After my mother died in the flu epidemic of 1919, he took my brothers, sister, and me to live on a ranch in Saskatchewan where he worked as a blacksmith. While we lived there, the rancher's wife introduced my father to socialism, which she had studied at the Rand School of Socialism in New York. Before long, my father was reading *Das Kapital*, and by the time he left the ranch in 1924, he was ready for the Revolution, in which he could play a more interesting role than that of being a father to his four children.

For the next few years, all his time and money went to the party. My brothers, my sister, and I were merely bystanders to the part he was playing in history, and we became, of necessity, independent, self-reliant brats. In 1927, my father became a full-time functionary of the party, and shortly after we moved to Winnipeg. I had left school by then and eventually found a job working first in the laundry and then as nursing student at St. Joseph's Hospital in North Winnipeg.

The time flew by. Nursing students worked twelve hours a day in the hospital, six and a half days a week–with classes at night–all for spuds, beans, and twelve dollars a year. Life was full, work was hard, and no one listened much to the news of the outside world. When the stock market crashed in 1929, we heard none of the bang.

Near the end of my second year of training, my family moved to Toronto, and I was cut off from news of them, too. Then in December 1931, the newspapers began screaming that eight Communists had been arrested for sedition. I didn't even know what sedition was, but everyone knew that my father was one of those arrested. Every morning the headlines of the *Winnipeg Free Press* proclaimed the sins of Tom Ewen and the others.

The trial seemed to take a very long time, and the press made the most of it. Then one morning the paper announced, "Five Years in Kingston Penitentiary for Notorious Reds." A lot of people probably slept better for a few nights, at least until it became clear that the notorious Reds were going to appeal their cases.

It was in the middle of this appeal that I arrived in Toronto to say goodbye to my family. My younger brother and sister attended the sessions in Osgoode Hall, but wild horses couldn't have dragged me there. The outcome of the appeal did not alter the decision handed down by the lower court. Five years in the federal pen became a reality for Tom Ewen. But I was most concerned about Isobel and Bruce. They, however, cheerfully announced that they could take care of themselves. Isobel said that a friend had given her a job in a coffee shop from seven in the morning till six-thirty at night. Young Bruce was to work in a print shop for another friend from four till midnight after school. They earned the grand sum of five dollars a week. My bourgeois mind questioned how the good comrades who owned restaurants and print shops could afford such "luxuries."

My brother and sister were quite jolted to learn that I was going to China. In the end, though, they were delighted at my prospects and not a little excited. They eagerly urged me to write every day about all the wonderful things I would see and learn.

So it was that as my father became the guest of the Government of Canada in Kingston, my friends and I journeyed to Vancouver, British Columbia, where we boarded the *White Empress* bound for the Orient.

Two days out of Vancouver the roughness of winter disappeared, and we soon changed our drab winter dresses for summer whites and colours. The sea seemed to take on a much deeper blue; the white-caps were a dazzling rinse white. Schools of porpoises frolicked along side the ship–quite a thrill for drylanders who had never seen masses of water larger than small lakes.

Five days brought us to Honolulu and the Islands. Polynesian friends of Father Vincent Schrempp, who was accompanying us, came aboard to take us ashore. We toured the town and its environs in their large Rolls-Royce, then drove to their palatial home for supper. The luau proved to be more than we bargained for. It was a real feast, with *poi* even. Such opulence took our collective breath away.

Father Vincent remained with our hosts while we went off to a dance with escorts who were most polite and correct. I am sure that they did not forget for a second that we were planning to be missionaries. As midnight drew near we thanked them for the lovely time and made our way back to the ship.

As we walked along the dock, several of the ship's officers insisted that we could not leave Honolulu without walking along Waikiki Beach. At that time there were two hotels on the beach, the Moana and the Royal Hawaiian. The officers took us dancing at the Moana Hotel, which was rather a posh spot in those days. "We Won't Go Home Till Morning" turned out to be our song that night, because the sailors said we couldn't leave this lovely spot without watching the sun rise, which we did from a big rock under the palm trees. Some missionaries, I concluded to myself.

We were back on the *Empress* for breakfast, and at eleven in the morning, to the tune of "Aloha Oe," we glided seaward, while the romantic passengers cast their garlands into the salt-chuck. Legend says that if the flowers float shoreward then the wearer will someday return to the islands. I wasn't sure that I wanted to come back so I kept and cherished even the droopiest ginger blossoms for days.

As we approached Yokohama, the smell of rotten fish became more unmistakable and offensive. Japanese customs men came aboard and approved our passports quickly. They did not seem to be particularly interested in why we were going to China.

Our next port of call was Kobe. We were most impressed by the dress of the populace. All manner of garb, some western, some Oriental, and some half and half–like a western coat over kimono and sandals–was evident. Kobe was a very short stop; it was a military area which contained large coking ovens and shipyards. The smell of the place was no different from Yokohama and it was incredibly dirty and unkempt. However, we visited a teahouse where we sat on the floor and ate with chopsticks, dipping the piping hot food into a small cup with a beaten-up raw egg in it. We had a hilarious time. The geisha girl wanted to sit on Father Vincent's lap. He protested vigorously–and the geisha then danced the Cherry Dance for him. He blushed all over, pretending he didn't understand the implication.

Soon it was over; the lights flickered away in the distance. The next two days would see the journey over, as we neared the China coast. Or perhaps the journey had just begun.

Shanghai, called the Paradise of Adventures, was one of the greatest cities on earth in 1933. It was a monument to foreign imperialism and a bastion of degradation and humiliation for a whole nation of Chinese people. Its great skyscrapers and fine edifices were built by slave labour working for oil companies, banks, and shipyard companies. Along the street from the jetty was the beautiful Garden Park displaying a bilingual sign on its iron gates: "Chinese and dogs not allowed." Across the street was the British Consulate, outside whose gates British soldiers stood sentry with rifles with bayonets.

Father Vincent was met by one of the missionaries from Shantung. He had arranged our lodgings at the home of Madame Bedard who ran a *pensionne* in the French concession. We found that Frenchtown was not too different from the international concession, except that the tricolour floated from public buildings and the policeman on the corner spoke French. Beyond the rickshaw men and the beggars on the street, we had no contact with the Chinese people. Our Shanghai stay was too short, even though we did range far and wide on our own.

Father Vincent dropped in on us after five days to say that passage had been booked for us on a Japanese coastal steamer, the *Darien Maru*, bound for Tsingtao in Shantung province. We had hoped to go by rail on the Blue Express and see some of the countryside, and so it was with reluctance that we boarded the ship, which was spotless as only Japanese boats are, but still had the aroma of rotten fish and laundry. The Yellow Sea was calm for the time of the year, and the *Darien Maru* had a smooth run.

Early on the second morning we tied up at Tsingtao, a city of white houses and red-tiled roofs. Jackpines grew everywhere on the rolling hills. Two of the missionaries met us with an elegant carriage drawn by a not-so-elegant horse and a mule. The carriage was one of those open contraptions with seats facing each other, doors on either side and iron steps to match. If the threadbare carpet and upholstery were any indication, the vehicle had seen better and more prosperous days.

We might have been royalty as we rode from the dock to the train depot. Hundreds of kids trailed along, with their hands out, shouting, "Give, give. I am hungry! May you become rich." Begging, we were told, was an honourable profession, and most beggars belonged to a union or organization to which the daily take was paid and from which they received food, rags, and a place to sleep, as well as protection from the police. We boarded the Tsingtao-Tsinan Railway about nine o'clock. It did not usually run on schedule but that day it did, which meant that by evening we were at the mission compound at Changtien, which was to be our home for a while. It was as squalid a town as the imagination could conceive. The smells we inhaled had, I am sure, never been whiffed by any westerner before.

Changtien was the home of most of the Chang clan. Most families were related in some manner. The oldest of the Changs owned and operated the local tannery, three shifts a day, seven days a week. The smell of rotting pelts and the chemicals used to tan the hides pervaded the town. It was a common joke that if your dog or cat disappeared, his hide would most certainly turn up on the tannery walls within a week.

Rose, Agnes, Father Vincent, and I were met at the mission gates by an American nurse, Bertha Buehler, and the resident priest, Father Phillip. The compound was enclosed by a six-foot brick fence topped with three strands of barbed wire. The gatekeeper had a small house at the front gate from which he scrutinized every caller and salesman.

Inside the compound, tree-lined walks and rose bushes gave the drab buildings a facade of splendour. Across from the gatehouse a series of rooms, one of which opened onto the street, made up the dispensary where patients came to have eyes cared for, dressings changed, or minor injuries looked after by the nurse, Bai Hu Shih.

Dr. Scherr and Miss Bai were busy caring for patients when we arrived. They welcomed us with much enthusiasm, the kind one rarely receives from strangers. It was almost embarrassing. Dr. Scherr could not speak English fluently, and we could not speak German or Chinese, but through Bai Hu Shih we managed to communicate. The doctor came to the mission from Tsinan once a week. This was all the time he could spare from his full-time duty at the St. Joseph's Hospital there.

The evening meal at the mission was a community affair. Since newcomers were a rarity in this part of the country, even the local mandarin and city officials arrived to welcome the head of the missions, Father Vincent.

When it comes to making *faux pas* I'm an expert. The more I try to remedy the damage, the worse it becomes. That evening I started off by asking if the doctor was also a missionary.

"What do you mean?" asked Bertha.

"Nothing, except does he preach as well as do missionary work?" I replied.

"Oh, no," Bertha ventured, "that would not be proper." Apparently there was the division of labour–the missionary didn't bind the sores of Lazarus's body, only the sores of his spirit. Besides, I was told, the missionaries had far too much to do as they had extensive parishes to visit. Sometimes they also had schools where they taught Chinese boys and girls who might themselves become missionaries.

In those first days we settled down to learn the language, which in itself amounted to a prolonged major operation. There was no way around this problem, for without the language of the native people, a missionary is like a man who is deaf and dumb. Isolation can be fatal. Besides learning ordinarily used characters, we were required to know Latin in order to learn Ku Ging Fadge, a form of Chinese that had been instituted by an Italian bishop for use among students and foreigners who were too stupid to cope with traditional Chinese characters. By using some Russian and Greek letters along with the Latin, the bishop had compiled an alphabet of sorts, which could be used to write Chinese without much hardship.

Our teacher was a Chinese gentleman with a good

scholastic background. He was very polite, but he didn't have the ability to arouse enthusiasm in his pupils. I learned three or four phrases, along with "please" and "thank you" and then I started to teach myself. Everybody I met became my teacher. "What is this called?" I would ask, pointing to a dog, a horse, or any object near at hand. "*Je shih shemo*?" The Chinese people are a most polite race. If you make a mistake they do not laugh at you (to your face anyway) but will correct your error and advise you how to pronounce correctly. I am sure they had some private laughs at my early attempts.

At the end of two months my oral Chinese was passable, and it was fun. I even went to the marketplace when it was in full swing and managed to dicker with the merchants.

We were soon put to work in the dispensary looking after out-patients and going to the homes of very sick patients and caring for them in their own environment. Chinese houses were mostly built of bricks made of straw and mud with several inches of thatched roof. Door frames and doors were made of wood. Window frames were also constructed of wood but contained no glass unless the man who owned the house was very wealthy. Instead, the frames were usually covered with white rice paper. Rooms were built end-to-end around a courtyard. The kitchen was liable to be a lean-to, the stove sunk into the earth with an iron cauldron for boiling rice or millet. Over to the side was a large box with bellows to keep the fire going.

Tables and chairs and eating utensils were usually kept in the room where there was also a *kong*–a Chinese bed. These *kongs* were about two feet off the floor, above two or four square openings in the floor where the housewife might put a fire on chilly winter nights. The *kong* was covered with a fancy quilt and pillows were stacked on the end. To sleep on a clean, warm *kong* was the ultimate in luxury.

Hens, dogs, and sometimes the family pig wandered through the house. They followed the children who romped around at will till they were seven years old, when they were considered to have reached the age of reason and were put to work. The girls were quite young when they were taught to sew, weave cloth, or make shoes. In fact, foot binding was still prevalent among some of the people, although Christian parents no longer allowed it. A woman with bound feet could not walk but hobbled on her heels. Even when she stood erect she teetered back and forth and was never still. The enslavement of women started at an early age.

I had once thought that mission schools were enlightened institutions–enlightened and more liberal–but as time went on I found they were not. A girls' school could be merely a name for a foundling home. The girls did the cleaning, the sewing, and washing around the compound. The only teaching done was catechism because few of the teachers had themselves gone to school. A lot of the girls somehow taught themselves enough characters to be able to read a newspaper but in general it was considered unnecessary to educate girls. What would they do with it? One did not need an education to have children or feed pigs on a farm. The girls used to look at me in astonishment when I asked, "Why not?"

When these girls were married there was no bride price as such, but the prospective husband was expected to make a sizable donation to the church. Either way it was the same, to my thinking.

The only recognition a woman got as a person in feudal China was when her children were grown and she became someone's mother-in-law. This invested her with the authority to bully, beat, curse her daughter-in-law, and generally make the young wife as miserable as she could possibly contrive. Woe to the young wife who did not have sons, for she was soon discarded for a concubine.

At the dispensary we treated everything from ingrown toenails to leprosy. Around Changtien there were a number of blind lepers, who tapped their staffs and jangled their begging cups. When one came along the lane, everybody in the vicinity ran, including the dogs.

One old man passed the dispensary door regularly, crying, "*Ko lian wo*!" (Have mercy on me!) His feet were wrapped in layers of dirty rags and his trousers were so dirty that they no longer clung to his bony thighs. When the sun shone brightly and warmly he wore no jacket; but he always wore the same headgear–a white turban-like cap. White was the colour of mourning. Only the dead were wrapped in white. Lepers were to all intents and purposes dead, having no home or material wealth.

I asked Dr. Scherr if we couldn't look at the leper as a patient.

"Yes, but we must wear rubber gloves and see him outside," he explained. "If we allow him in the waiting room no patients will ever come back here. They would be too afraid of contamination."

The man had no fingers on one hand and the sores on his body were nauseating, especially the ones on his backside. Dr. Scherr asked him a lot of questions and concluded that the sores might not actually be from leprosy but from malnutrition.

In summer, the days got hotter and the smell of the tannery more ghastly. Shantung, where the mission was located, was at that time reputed to be the most prosperous and richest province in all of China. Many families grew fruit trees in their fields. Apricots and cherries were easily available. Bertha cautioned us not to eat raw fruit without washing it first in pot permanganate, lest we come down with cholera, or at the very least dysentery, which is endemic in the interior of the province during July and August. This advice fell mostly on deaf ears.

By midsummer, we were ready to move on to our next post at a new dispensary at Kiang Kia, north of the Yellow River about sixty miles from Changtien in the country of Wu Ting. Agnes, Rose, and I were moved, bag and baggage, in the new Ford truck that had recently been acquired by the mission to facilitate its work.

On our way to Kiang Kia, we saw wheat being harvested. The crop was sown in November and harvested in June, stock by stock. It was then put through a primitive separator: an ox or donkey dragged a stone weighing several hundred pounds over it on a packed earth floor. The women cleaned off the straw and the chaff, and swept up the grain into large shallow baskets. Then the grain was winnowed. The wheat was thrown into the wind, which blew away excess sand and chaff, leaving only the golden grain caught in the bottom of the basket. Not a single grain was wasted. Heaven help the hen who stepped in to snitch a kernel.

The farmer's land had to yield at least three crops a year in order to sustain his family. It was a hard life and everybody worked during harvests and planting. After the wheat crop, sweet potatoes, vegetables, and *gauliang* (maize) were planted. Cash crops of melons, peanuts, tobacco, and cotton brought the farmer a little extra money. In this country, crops were of low yield, so the peasants were not prosperous.

The resident missionary at Kiang Kia, Father Edwin, had built a three-room house consisting of a large bedroom, a living room, and a kitchen. The dispensary consisted of three rooms along the outside of the lot. In the centre was a big courtyard with a tall elm tree just outside the door.

The new dispensary opened its doors in the hottest part of the season at a time when many babies fell ill and died from dysentery. Small wonder. Hygiene was unknown, and the people were too poor to buy diapers for the babies. The little ones had a sack of sand put on their bottoms. When the sand became too wet or soiled a new lot was put on. Small toddlers ran around wearing a "fig leaf," exposed to flies and dirt of all kinds. A fig leaf is a piece of cloth, usually diamond shaped, just big enough to cover the front nakedness. It is supported by a halter and two side strings, which tie at the back like an apron.

At Kiang Kia there was a boys' school and a girls' school. The children had never had health checks. We soon established Monday morning roll calls, at which we examined hair, ears, throat, and teeth. Daily vitamins and extra food were given.

Father Edwin was a little surprised when the three of us confronted him with the possibility of beginning a pre-school. The village contained thirty-five to forty children under three years of age who could use vitamins and milk. They were all children of local Christians. It took a lot of persuasion, but soon the pre-school became a reality.

One day we had an artist of sorts come to our house to make some posters for our public health campaign against flies. There were no sanitation or public health programmes. The government simply wasn't responsible for anything. It was when we were in the middle of paints and paper that we had our first maternity case.

Usually babies were delivered by midwives, because the farm women were too shy to come to us. This time, a man came to the outer gate and asked if a nurse could please come to Mr. Wong's house. His wife had been in labour for four days but had not yet delivered. Why didn't they call on us earlier? we asked. They feared we might not come, but now they felt it was a dire necessity and we could not refuse. They had horses to take us the five miles.

Rose and I got the obstetrical instruments, a little anaesthesia, and bundled up with some misgivings and fear. Neither of us had ever delivered a baby before. We knew how to tie the cord and express the placenta but that was the extent of our training. The nearest doctor was sixty miles away—*if* he were at Changtien.

The trip to the patient did not take long. We were led into the courtyard, past an unco-operative, growling dog held in leash by a teenage boy. First the master of the house insisted that we have tea. Not being very polite people, we insisted on seeing the patient. We were escorted through two courtyards to a small, foul-smelling room where the patient seemed to be in advanced labour. Three old midwives sat on the back of the *kong*. They were all dressed in black and each seemed to be well over sixty-five years old. They looked at us curiously as we listened to the fetal heart with our one and only stethoscope. Everything seemed to be all right. We took the woman's measurements with our instruments and did a rectal examination.

Rose looked up for a second. A crowd had gathered and there seemed to be fifty people gaping open-mouthed at us, watching everything we were doing. In her very best Chinese Rose told them all to go home and get pregnant themselves; then we would do the same for them. Whereupon she calmly closed the door in their faces. The room was so dark we needed our flashlights.

After a conference, we decided that the patient had not

reached the end of the first stage of labour. Perhaps a little nembutal might help this along. Rose went back to Kiang Kia to help Agnes with the morning's work, while I stayed with the patient. In the meantime I was served breakfast–slices of fat pork, salted eggs, steamed bread, and millet soup.

At lunchtime Agnes rode in on a small pony just in time to give a little chloroform to help the patient deliver a bouncing baby boy. The placenta came on schedule, and everything went well.

I wrapped the placenta in paper to burn, but the three old midwives suddenly came to life, protesting that no one burned a placenta, ever. Mr. Wong explained that in China the placenta was sold to a druggist when it was dry; then it was ground into a powder and used for female troubles. This was a very old Chinese remedy, he assured us, and a very effective one. In his most polite manner Mr. Wong also asked us to be sure to close the openings of the umbilical cord. His wife had had two normal children previously but both had died of tetanus some six days after birth, either because the openings in the cord were left open, or because of contaminated instruments.

One of us rode out every day to do the umbilical dressing till the cord fell off, and everybody was happy. Mr. Wong would not be convinced that only contamination could infect the umbilical cord. He assured us that his household was known to be the purest and cleanest in that part of the country.

Some days later a great commotion took place outside the big gate, with musicians and many people dressed in their best garments. The Wongs had come to honour their benefactors, namely us, for the service done them in delivering their small son safely. Their gifts consisted of many fruits, native wines of North Shantung, and an ornate silver shield engraved with nice compliments about the church and especially the nurses. The missionary said they were giving us great face; indeed, the house of Wong overdid itself. The rules of Chinese etiquette forbade that we accept more than two items of food or wine. To acknowledge the "face" that the Wongs had bestowed on our unworthy abode we had to invite them to a banquet. The number one boy at the mission house stepped in and took charge of all the arrangements so that the acknowledgement would be adequate.

Strictly speaking, no woman ever attended a formal Chinese dinner, so after having a spot of wine, we left the men to their games. Funny world: Mrs. Wong had the baby and her menfolk had all the glory.

The Wong baby marked the beginning of a new era at the dispensary. From then on we delivered many babies, but our pre-natal care clinic fell flat on its face. We were ahead of ourselves in this part of the country. Pre-natal care is considered by women and their husbands as unnecessary. You carry the baby or you drop it, is the belief. We were appalled at the failure of the native population to institute measures that we, at least, felt were for their own benefit.

We also instituted a well-baby clinic, but it also died a natural death. The peasants could not see why they should bring a baby into the clinic when there was apparently nothing wrong with the child. Vitamins and weight gain were of questionable value, they argued; if the child grew it would also gain weight. However, we got enough sick ones, most suffering from malnutrition; babies with swollen bellies and thin, toothpick legs and arms.

As we expanded, Father Edwin decided we should take two or three girls into the dispensary to help with dressings, care for sick patients in the home, even deliver babies. Our first apprentice from the girls' school was Hsu Ying, a farmer's daughter from Loling near the Hopeh border. Hsu Ying's father wanted to sell her in marriage to a well-to-do merchant in Loling. The contract had been made, with the marriage to take place the next spring. Hsu Ying, who had made up her mind that there was to be no such wedding, was procrastinating as much as possible. She was a bright girl and knew what she wanted, and that did not include a mother-in-law.

Just before Christmas her father came to see her. He had intended to take his daughter home, but when he saw her at work he was very impressed. Dressed in her white gown with her organza veil over her hair she looked radiantly healthy.

We invited him to tea and accepted gifts of apples and pears from his farm in Loling. Hsu Ying gave her father her three months' wages, keeping out just enough for a new white gown so that she would have an extra uniform. Her father said nothing about the betrothal and returned to Loling, seeming quite happy. After all, hadn't his daughter given him a hundred dollars, asking nothing in return? In old China only sons made money for their father.

Our first Christmas in China was a big event. As the feast day approached, Agnes and Rose got a little more homesick. A week before, the workmen built a life-sized stable and crib outside the church. The figures of Mary, Joseph, and the baby were life-sized wooden carvings with Oriental features. They had black hair, almond eyes, and olive skin. The baby Jesus was swaddled in Oriental styling, his hair tufted with red yarn. The spaces in between the tufts remained bare, as though his head had been shaved-just like the little Chinese babies. The two tufts of hair that stick out from either side of a child's head are to enable the good spirits to extricate him from trouble or impending danger.

Christmas day was open house at the mission. Christians came from far and near to chat with the missionary, and guests arrived late into the evening bearing gifts of food and wine. Etiquette demanded that each guest be urged to stay for dinner, which was served in ten courses at the school. Two fattened pigs were slaughtered and the cooks had barbecued them. Wine and fruit with a steamed pudding not unlike Christmas cake were first on the menu. Great vats of steaming rice and sautéed vegetables and chickens helped to fill the emptiness of the guests who had travelled a long way. There were piles of *jutsai bodtses* (chiotses), which was my favourite food: chopped pork with spices cased in dough and steamed. At last count we had been given fifteen bottles of *bai gar* (Chinese whiskey), an overproof alcohol made from grain. We could have started a well-stocked store with all the gifts brought to the mission house.

Our first New Year passed practically unnoticed. In 1934, we had a great deal of work ahead of us. Hsu Ying was studying to be a catechist, having learned all the nursing that was required of her. She knew how to deliver a child, tie the cord properly, and perform the basics of post-natal care for the mother and child. Soon she would be leaving the dispensary; in her place we were to get two catechists who wanted to learn a little about *kau bing* (looking after the sick). The girls would be going towards the north coast of Shantung, where there were no hospitals or schools.

After the holiday interval, Dr. Scherr and his assistant, Dr. Liu, visited us. We had quite a few cases for them. One patient in particular caused us a great deal of concern. Her left leg was covered with the most revolting-looking sores, more like a series of ulcers. The leg did not respond to treatment either. The doctors laughed at our anxiety. "Why, that's tuberculosis of the skin. Give her gallons of orange juice, cod liver oil, and other vitamins, along with plenty of good nourishing food. In a couple of years the sores will go away by themselves."

She received as much treatment as we were able to give her. Her husband, however, did not consider her worth the extra load on the grocery bill. Before she left, we gave her as many vitamins as we could, along with extra dressings and ointments.

During our conference with the doctors, a middle-aged farmer came to the dispensary with his left hand wrapped in dirty rags. His mule had bitten him three weeks earlier, severing most of his hand except for the tendons. From the smell and flies it might have happened three months ago. As the process of unwrapping continued, the stench got stronger. Finally when we reached the hand, we saw white maggots crawling all over it. What had been his thumb and first two fingers was just a black blob of rot hanging by glistening white tendons. Dr. Liu clipped and anchored the tendons at the wrist. He instructed us not to put anything other than a vaseline dressing on the wound, for under the layer of maggots was granulating tissue. Both doctors thought the man should go to the hospital for a week or so. The patient replied that he had no money to go to Tsinan.

"I will take you in my car," said Dr. Scherr. The man could not believe his ears; he had never been in a car of any kind. He went home to think about it. He returned next morning to inspect the doctor's car to see if it was safe, or if it would steal his soul. Peasants believed that anything they did not understand would somehow steal their souls, making it impossible for them to function as humans. If a child fell off a donkey or a chair or just fell, his mother or another adult quickly picked up a handful of earth, smeared his head with it, and muttered, *"Ohme two fu."* This was done three times to make sure his soul was still with him–a sort of "God bless you."

Finally, the patient, deciding that the little Ford was safe enough, sat by the car most of the night so Dr. Scherr would not go without him. When the car finally left Kiang Kia, all his kinfolk came to see him off. They looked the car over and made remarks about its reliability, and about what made it go. They also brought the patient bundles of food. One might have thought he was going to the moon, and that indeed there was a famine there!

The Chinese New Year gave us a small respite from patients. No one had time to think of pains and aches with all the celebrations. For weeks before the actual day, farm women were baking shortbread, cookies, pigs in blankets, roasting fowl, or making *goa* (a delicious millet pudding with dates and brown sugar, which is wrapped in a palm leaf for the steamer and eaten hot). The whole celebration lasted fifteen days and nights. The day before New Year the women pasted candies over the mouths of the kitchen gods so that the gods would not be able to say mean things about the household where they resided for the last year. New gods and Weifang posters went up at the New Year. Weifang, a very old native art form belonging to the Weifang area in Shantung province, has unique styles of painting and vivid colour. Rose and Agnes decided we had better have a kitchen god, too, so they took an old newspaper photograph of me and glued sticky gum drops over my mouth and stuck me up over the stove in the kitchen.

The momentous hour of the dawning of the New Year arrived, heralded by thundering firecrackers and bells and drums. Each neighbour went to the next to wish him all the good things he wanted, have a cup of wine with him, and, if he owed him any money, to repay it. The children were given money in lieu of gifts for there were no fabulous toys and games for youngsters as there were in Canada. How very much these children have missed–or have they? If I ever had reason to think my childhood dreary, I no longer harboured such thoughts. But no child ever grows up with as much spoiling as a Chinese child does.

The winter days were cold, and there was usually a powdery layer of snow on the ground. We had no central heating and could not buy fuel in large quantity. We all wore dark-blue satin padded gowns made in the traditional style, with slits to the knee. We might have passed for Chinese except for our big feet, which were a source of amusement to the local women.

We did get electricity that winter, however, and now had three lights: one at the front gate, one in the kitchen, and one in the living room. They fascinated the visitors even though they dimmed occasionally when the gas ran low in the powerhouse generator. Old ladies declared that it was the work of the Devil, for who but Old Nick could make fire run down a piece of wire into a glass.

After the New Year's celebrations, things were a bit dull for a while, until the days got warmer. The days just before spring are the beginning of silk-worm cultivation. Mulberry trees sprout early but are kept defoliated to feed the silk worms. The pink cocoons are stored in granaries and empty spaces from the year before. At the first warmth of spring they begin to hatch. The housewife usually empties out a room to make way for the young worms.

I walked into a friend's house to have a look at the worms in action but the housewife shooed me out because the smell of soap on my hands and clothes would kill her worms.

"Don't you ever wash your hands or face during this season?" I asked, like an oaf.

My friend looked at me as if I were senseless. She shook her head. "A little topsoil never hurt anyone, at least not me."

Day and night she tended these wigglers, feeding them continuously on fresh mulberry leaves. When she decided they were mating, she frantically stripped branches and made trellises for them to crawl up. There the female made a cocoon of finest silk in a bobbin-shaped elongated ball.

The harvesting of silk thread gave relatives a chance to come and visit, learn all the local gossip, and have a few free meals. Unravelling and making the thread usually fell to the eldest and most experienced female of the clan. A large cauldron of water was brought to a boil and the largest of the cocoons were immersed in it. A pair of deft hands, aided by chopsticks, grasped the tiny pink filament, unravelling it to the very end, while another person took the filament and wound it on a small wheel like a spinning bobbin. A good day's work for several women consisted of two or three large hanks of silvery shining silk thread.

Silk thread is a most amazing product, possessing great softness and strength. It will not break if you bite it, nor will it come to pieces if you chew it. Shantung silk, as it is made in the homes of the peasants, is not unlike canvas. It can be bleached, scrubbed, and generally mistreated, yet it retains its texture, weight, colour, and beauty.

There were now five women working in our dispensary so once again the mission directors decided it was time to expand. Since I was more fluent than either Rose or Agnes, there was no question about it; I was the one to go. Before Easter, I was notified that I was to move to an old Li village, some thirty miles to the east along the Yellow River, called Chu Li Chang.

CHAPTER TWO

In Chu Li Chang, people were somewhat more prosperous than those in Kiang Kia. The children looked healthier and chubbier, the women were better dressed. There was also a good-sized public school there, open to all ages, and supported by the local population. These schools could in no way be compared with the great institutions of learning in our country. They were no more than mud huts, with thatched roofs, while benches and desks were of rough lumber, mostly hand-hewn and constructed. A small blackboard sufficed as equipment, and each child had his own slate and chalk. There were about sixty students from ages six to twenty. The lone teacher was something of a wizard, for he copied his own textbooks, which were sewn together with cotton thread. However, he was also steeped in Confucianism, which even in this never-changing China was out of date.

In the middle of town stood a Buddhist temple where a holy man lived by himself, keeping the place in order. At each meal he would go out with his begging cup to seek his meal, which he took back to the temple and ate in the doorway of the shrine where the great Buddha was enthroned. The old man was so thin he looked like a bag of bones. I do not think that he was very old, but with such strict self-denial and fasting, there was no way of knowing his actual age. He was not only a holy man but, I found, a very wise man as well. He was as kind and gentle as he was ragged. Even in winter he wore no shoes and had only one suit of clothes to his name. He refused to accept another for he believed that having two of one item of clothing compromised him in some way.

The Catholic mission compound was located at the southernmost end of town near an open area used as a marketplace. Market days were Tuesdays and Saturdays. Consequently, on those days, there was a hubbub till well after sundown. At these markets cheap produce of all kinds was available to those with money. Cloth, buttons, thread, soap, Japanese aspirins, cosmetics, socks, and knee-high silk stockings in the wildest shades were sold.

I had been in Chu Li Chang about three months when I found a young woman named Li Ling who wanted to be my helper, but the resident missionary, Father Shu, refused to allow Li Chih Lan, another girl who acted as my aide, to be dismissed. Dismissal would have meant a loss of face for her parents, who were prominent Christians in this area. We kept her on as a helper, therefore; but also allowed Li Ling to work as an aide.

At the end of June when the weather was unbearably hot and the air filled with all manner of flying insects, Doctors Scherr and Liu came to visit the dispensary. They thought that since the place had only recently opened they would be in for a little rest. We sent for our most ailing patients and the doctors started to work in our makeshift operating room, removing tumours, treating three pairs of club feet for three toddlers, and examining people with cataracts and eye troubles of every kind–glaucoma, trachoma, and others I had never seen before. Many people in the area suffered from trachoma. The eyes became red and swollen, and the inside of the lids looked as though grains of sand lodged just under the mucous membrane.

We kept the doctors busy for the whole of their stay with us. I think they were glad to return to their regular schedule in the end.

My first maternity case in Chu Li Chang came on the heels of a thundering evening downpour of rain. It was the same story as the Wong case earlier–long labour and local midwives who just couldn't deliver the baby. I took both of my aides with me. They were anxious to learn, but I think they went into a state of mild shock; neither had ever seen a baby born.

The village where the patient lived was three miles away.

When we arrived, all the relatives had gathered in expectation that the patient would die. Two midwives were squatting on the floor beside the patient, who was seated on a small stool with her back up against the *kong*. Like the midwives of Kiang Kia, these were dressed in black and made snide remarks about children doing the work of adults.

When I examined the patient I nearly died myself. Here was a problem I was not prepared to face. A small hand protruded from the mouth of the vagina. With every contraction the mouth gaped a little more, and the grotesque tongue-like hand got a little blacker. The hand was cold, swollen, and the tiny bones broken. No fetal heart sounded, so there was no hope of a living child. I put on gloves and started the task of putting the hand back. It seemed a very long time before it suddenly went back. Dousing my gloves and myself and everything around me with soapy lysol solution, I reached into the vagina and pulled down the feet.

Soon it was over. Li Ling tied the cord, cut it, and handed the small body to the midwives. The placenta came free with no trouble and was hung up for the witch doctor. Earlier the witch doctor had been there leaving a charm of chicken bones, red feathers, and yellow papers in a small green bag. These were representatives of the mother's life and soul and they were supposed to be returned to the witch doctor with money if she recovered. I took them outside. The dogs were hanging around waiting. I asked Li Chih Lan if they would feed on the corpse of the baby. She said, "Yes. If they don't get to it here, they will dig it out of the straw matting in the field."

I left my patient sleeping, with a shot of chloral hydrate after her ergotomine injection. On the way home I started to worry that she might get an infection. My visions of the lady dying of some germs I had given her bothered me all the next night and day. I took my bad temper out on the missionary, Father Shu, who had just come home from many weeks of visitations at the outlying parishes. After I finished raving about all the inadequacies he calmly said, "Well, this is China. This is not the strangest of things you will see while you are here." The greater fear kept shouting at me; post partum infection from my own and the midwives' dirt.

Since I had heard nothing from the patient in nearly three days, I decided to ride out and see her. She wasn't where I had left her but was out in the field working. Her husband was astonished that I was concerned about his wife, who, he declared, was as strong as a horse. He could not afford to keep her in idleness; and because she did not have a child to suckle, she must earn her keep. I excused myself and fled.

When I told Father Shu, he said, "Well, the meek inherit the earth."

"Wrong, Father, they only inherit the dirt," I assured him. He looked as though I had punched him in the nose.

In order to teach some simple ideas of hygiene to our patients, we decided to put some sanitation propaganda on the bare white walls of the dispensary. Li Chih Lan said her brother did some fine art work, so we enlisted his talents to paint some pictures. After much discussion about what was needed and some instructions he began to work. The wall opposite the door depicted the stages of growth of the fly, which carried a heavy load of germs on its feet. Characters explained that these feet carried sickness for someone. We ultimately went into the fly business, buying a hundred flies for five *cash* from any boy or girl. A *cash* was worth about one-tenth of a Chinese cent. Certainly no child would ever get rich at the going rate, but a number of lads were enterprising enough to snare their share of the loot, which in turn supported the candy man.

During the next few months Li Ling and I delivered many babies. She was becoming most proficient as a midwife. In the evenings she and I translated a few chapters about prenatal care and delivery from my textbooks on obstetrics.

With the coming of fall another young woman came to the dispensary for training. I could never remember her Chinese name, Soong, so we just called her Mie Mie–little sister. She was very intelligent and worked hard learning all the small lessons that Li Ling had put down in characters. Soon she accompanied us on calls. Li Chih Lan stayed in the dispensary. Her father hadn't been pleased that she went with us to a maternity case.

Li Ling came bouncing into work one frosty September morning, asking me if I had heard the latest news. In fact, she said, everyone had known for some time. Li Chih Lan was leaving us to get married. The matchmaker had arranged what her father called a good marriage with a well-to-do merchant in a neighbouring county. The prospective bridegroom was much older than Chih Lan, and she had never seen him, which we didn't believe and we teasingly told her so. We were not surprised when a red envelope with many red ribbons was delivered to us. This meant that not only were we invited to the wedding, but a whopping big gift was due the bride.

The couple were first married very solemnly in the church at High Mass just like any other Christian couple. Chih Lan wore a red-satin, floor-length gown. Her skirt was exquisitely embroidered from hemline to waistline with butterflies, two peaches in an ever-present basket, countless fishes and birds. The butterflies symbolized true love, the peaches in a basket nuptial bliss, the fishes were for many sons, while the birds were for long life.

The celebration took place at the groom's home, where the bride was carried in a red sedan chair. The reluctant bride was expected to give her parents face by pretending not to want to get out of the chair. Chih Lan gave a good performance but couldn't hide the glint in her eye. In true Chinese fashion, three carriers presented our gifts from the dispensary–a Japanese tea set, two red-satin quilts, bolts of cloth, and a sum of money.

The couple pledged their marriage vows that evening kneeling before both sets of parents. The bridegroom had only his old father so Chih Lan would have no mother-in-law. They kotowed mightily to the floor many times. A kotow is a bow done from a kneeling position. Your eyes never roam above the feet directly in front of you. Kotows were fast disappearing from this old world.

The feast started with the red veil being removed from the bride's face and with the bride and groom drinking a toast together. The moment of truth for the groom was when the red veil was removed from the bride's face, and he learned whether he had a beauty or a beast. Chih Lan looked so beautiful and radiant that the relatives just breathed a big sigh. Everyone wished them happiness with *bai gar* (whiskey) and the feast began.

There was one custom in this part of China that I thought rather peculiar. When the bridal couple retired and the marriage was consummated, the groom threw the girl's trousers out the window. If they were stained with blood, he had a virgin and got what he paid for. The families were delighted, for many a bitter feud has started over a maidenhood–or lack of one.

One thing you never saw in China was a home for unwed mothers. It's not that there was no promiscuity; but most girls were married by the time they were fifteen, and therefore an unwed mother would be very young. If, however, a boy was born to an unmarried girl or woman, it was either left on the father's doorstep or given to a relative. If the child was a girl it was either left to die or the cord was not tied tight enough. All physical signs of pregnancy were studiously hidden. To have an illegitimate child was akin to having two left feet–big ones.

In Chu Li Chang village, I became a mother. One morning, very early, I awoke to the wails of an infant. Outside my door lay a small bundle of swaddled rags in which twenty coppers were rolled. If the recipient of the bundle accepted the customary coppers he or she was also required to accept the baby. My little girl lived only ten days. She died of tetanus, probably caused by dirty instruments used to cut the cord.

Before long we were getting ready for Christmas again. Father Shu asked if I wanted to go to Kiang Kia to spend the holidays with Rose and Agnes. I agreed, knowing that Soong and Li Ling could manage without me.

Going back to Kiang Kia was not unlike going home. The dispensary was still busy but Agnes and Rose were glad to see me. They were eager to hear about the new venture, new diseases, and the conditions I had discovered. We compared notes far into the night.

"Do you think you will like your new place?" Rose asked, wide-eyed.

Surely I was not to start out again! I had not heard anything about being moved. But long ago I recognized that life was a series of new beginnings, and I was prepared for almost anything.

The directors of the mission at Changtien apparently had a

meeting several weeks before in Kiang Kia and decided that I was to open a new dispensary to the northeast of Putai, far removed from the Yellow River and still farther removed from civilization. No one said anything, however, either before or during the holidays at Kiang Kia. I refused to discuss the matter. And so 1935 arrived.

Just before the Chinese New Year I returned to Chu Li Chang. Father Shu was not at home when I arrived. No one had used my little hut since my departure, although there was mail on the table. I took the dust cover off the bed, blew out the candle, and fell asleep. It seemed I had just dozed off when someone started pounding at the door. Blurry-eyed, I looked out on daylight and Li Ling's smiling face welcoming me back. She brought me breakfast while we pored over the records of the happenings during my absence. They had been busy and had managed well.

My move finally became official when the mission head returned from Hi Dja for a conference with Father Shu. He sent his number one boy to my hut to request my presence without delay. When I entered Father Shu's office, he bade me sit down and have some wine with him. The progress of the dispensary pleased everybody very much, especially the effects it had on the community at large. Father Shu felt that I was to be personally congratulated on my knowledge of China and my use of the language, which had prompted the directors at Changtien to indicate that they would be very pleased to have a dispensary opened at Kuotown, where Father Gu Xenfu was the missionary. This new dispensary was to open as soon as possible.

"What about supplies?" I asked, knowing that the dispensary at Chu Li Chang needed a new shipment of supplies and that it would be dangerous to deplete their stock any further.

It was arranged that I would go to Tsinan and buy supplies for Chu Li Chang and also for the new dispensary at Kuotown. I had never been to Tsinan before and was anxious to see this great walled city which was the home of the Governor of Shantung, Han Foo Chu, and his harem. A warlord by trade, he plundered and looted enough to allow him to live like a gentleman. In the traditional manner of a true Chinese gentleman, he had many concubines. His favourite, it was said, was a very blonde White Russian girl, fifteen years of age.

I spent nearly two weeks at St. Joseph's Hospital in Tsinan gathering supplies and helping in the operating rooms and in the out-patients department. I had had typhus inoculations, although Dr. Scherr was not sure that this would be prevalent around Kuotown. It was better to be safe than have any complex after-effects, if I survived the ordeal. After much study in pest control, especially lice, I was ready for the new adventure.

When I returned to the mission compound at Chu Li Chang the only instructions that greeted me were to proceed at once to my new assignment. I decided to take my time. It was early spring and I would probably be there awhile. I kept thinking of Kuotown, and worrying a little, too, for at age twenty-three, one's survival is most important.

One thing I knew after three years, I was not a missionary; I could not be, for the spirit of self-denial most certainly wasn't part of my make-up. To live like the missionaries one had to deny one's personal interests. All of this altruism confused me a little. I did things because I wanted to do them, it was that uncomplicated.

I took a stroll around the town, since I was sure I would not live at Chu Li Chang anymore. My friend the holy man was sitting in the outer doorway of his temple. He greeted me and enquired about my troubles. I told him I was leaving the village. He knew that already.

"You cannot live but one day at a time," he said. "In a few moments a whole way of life can change; therefore, you must learn to take one step at a time. You must be especially careful for your new work will take you to a very unpeaceful part of the country. Up there you will see a China that you never dreamed existed. Nothing will happen to you if you observe and be careful."

I bade him goodbye. His face seemed like an ancient parchment. His stringy beard and scraggly moustache were not white or grey, but instead, rather yellowish with age. I never saw him again. I heard he went on a pilgrimage to Lhasa and died along the way.

CHAPTER THREE

By June 1935 my preparations for the journey to Kuotown were completed, and our wagons finally pulled away from the familiar gates of the mission compound. The countryside grew increasingly bleak and unfriendly as we journeyed north. The ground became so poor that the crops of wheat, corn, and millet could hardly make their way through the rocks and clumps of dirt. The villages seemed desperate; peopled by gaunt humans and hungrier-looking dogs. Few children romped after the wagons as we passed through the towns.

Night had nearly closed in on us when we reached the dilapidated mission after a long journey. Kuotown was all huts and ruts, each hut more disreputable than the next. My new home was much less than anticipated, with only one room for eating, sleeping, and working. There was no door, so I had as much privacy as a goldfish in a bowl. The latticed window was covered with dark rice paper. At the end of the room was a *kong* on which I spread my bed roll. The old pot-bellied stove stood in the middle of the room, as cold as a night in December. The walls weren't even white-washed, although pictures of the Last Supper, Nativity, and the Pope hung on them. A table of sorts supported a pot of soya-bean oil with a wick floating in the centre. That was the only lighting available. I wondered how the Father had the gumption to stay in this poverty-stricken place.

I refused supper saying that I was not hungry, only very tired. I asked them all to go away and leave me alone to sleep.

"But you can't stay alone, there are bandits around here who might harm you," declared the number one boy from Chu Li Chang who had accompanied me on the journey.

"Bandits be damned," I said loudly and he vanished. Even though I *was* hungry, I climbed into bed and fell asleep, feeling very sorry for myself.

Suddenly it was morning, and I was awakened by two teachers who had come to take me on a tour. I thought they looked a little like their village, unkempt and pathetic.

"Where are all the children, the laughter-makers?" I asked them. "The town is very silent."

"Oh, there are few children here. People of these parts are riddled with syphilis, and have been for longer than anyone can remember," said the elder teacher.

The teachers called each other "sister," probably because they worked for the church. Sister Wong had a lot of grey in her thin hair. The line of her mouth was very hard, as though she had never known how to smile, as though life had been particularly bitter to her. Sister Kung also looked as if she had endured many hardships, but she was considerably younger than Sister Wong. The set of her face was also stern and severe; only when her eyes smiled did her face change. She became a different person.

I was given a tour of the school, which housed some thirty students. The teachers instructed them in religion, traditional characters, reading, and very elementary arithmetic. Confucius was much in evidence.

"Where does the missionary want the dispensary?" I finally asked.

"Oh, in the room where you sleep, of course. There is no other place for it," they insisted.

I pointed out that this was impossible. There was an empty room next door to mine that would serve. I told the sisters that I wanted glass in the windows, doors on both huts, and locks on the doors. The last straw was when I asked for fuel to cook with. Didn't I know that only the missionary had fuel? It was stacked in his house. Was there a key? Oh yes, the teachers had it but weren't keen on admitting me to their master's house. I told them I would take all the blame, and proceeded to help myself to his coal and wood, ready for a damned good fight with him when he arrived.

Patients were coming in even before the drugs and instruments were set up. Most were curious to know what the big boxes held. I needed a long table but there wasn't one to be had. Two smaller square ones had to suffice. The medicine cabinet was an old cupboard with doors that didn't quite fit. It also served to house instrument trays. The first things that were dispensed with were white uniforms–except for aprons. I would never manage the washing since the town wasn't blessed with an abundance of water.

I asked Sister Wong where I could find a young girl to help me around the dispensary.

"None of the girls around Kuotown would like to do this work. It might ruin their marriage prospects!" Sister Wong replied emphatically.

I had been at the mission several days when Father Gu Xenfu arrived. He looked less like a man of God than any I have ever seen. He was heavy set, with a florid and rather coarse face, and a receding hairline topped by a shock of carrot red hair that went down to his shoulders. He needed a haircut and a clean jacket. I made up my mind that I wasn't going to like this man from the start. He first tried speaking German to me, but when "Ja! Ja!" rang no bell he resorted to Chinese. He thought it would be better if the community understood what we had to say.

A week after I arrived in Kuotown I was asked to see a lady who was very ill. She was so ill, in fact, she was unconscious. Her face and hands were very swollen and discoloured. How did it happen? How long had she been sick? The answers were very evasive. Had the local sorcerer seen her? Yes, nearly a week ago. Did he make those marks on her face? They didn't know. I knew they weren't saying. I asked Sister Wong how the lady had managed to get bruises and welts all over her body. She pointed to the grist mill where she said they dragged the woman and beat her with willow switches to get the evil spirits out of her body. The sorcerer said this was the only way she would get better. Next morning the poor woman was dead.

As time went by, I got to know the missionary better and I found myself respecting him more each day. His compassion for people and their difficulties made him an outstanding person in the community. Kuotown grew on me as well. Soon I no longer noticed the ruts, the gloomy, tumbledown huts, or the lack of water.

Soon, too, I learned more about the local population. The farmers were all perennial optimists. With crop failures year after year, their hope that the next growing season would surely be the best yet was a little bit amazing. Each harvest saw them in debt a little more, but somehow they managed to beg, borrow, or hock some possessions to buy seed for the land. Then, to cause further headaches for them, highwaymen and bandits often stole what little they might acquire. The bandits invaded the town several nights a month shooting up the place. They made off with everything that could be stolen or bullied out of the inhabitants. They even carried away younger women, especially the better-looking ones, for themselves. At Kuotown the sentries kept us awake nearly every night by firing off their muzzle-loaders.

Early one morning in the fall of 1935, two husky lads dressed in military uniforms climbed over my wall, presented themselves at my door, and told me to get dressed. I was going to see a sick lady, they announced, and I was to take medicines with me. My first instinct was to scream bloody murder, but I knew no one would hear me; the missionary was away.

In a few minutes we were galloping like fools into the rising sun. Some five miles away a walled town appeared with soldiers on guard duty. The three horses galloped through the town gates to a compound of squalid huts, our destination. The soldiers took me into a white-washed shed where I was given tea before I went to see the boss-thief.

I was ushered into Hsu Sir's lofty presence by the two scoundrels who had brought me. The room was covered with the traditional trappings of a bridal chamber, including the earrings, bracelets, pretty shoes, and clothes belonging to either his wife or a concubine. The man looked like a pirate and swaggered a lot. He was tall and good featured except for his pock marks. His fur hat and fur-lined coat tied at the waist with a length of black cloth made him look like a Manchurian.

I bowed and asked, "General, what can I possibly do for you?"

He sensed that I was probably laughing at him, for he sized me up from head to foot and then said, a little contemptuously, "No wonder you became a nurse, you are too old and your feet too big for any man to want to marry you." His wife, he told me, was about five months pregnant. She had lost two pregnancies in her fifth and sixth months. He wanted me to do something to help save this one.

"What seems to be the trouble? Did she have syphilis?" I asked.

"Yes, how did you know?"

"Have you ever thought of giving her injections–needles?" I asked. That was my job. I told him there was special medication in Tsinan. I would write a letter asking for ampoules and instructions, and he could send one of his soldiers (out of uniform) to bring the drug back. He thought it over, not sure if it was safe. He didn't quite trust me, but finally decided he had no other alternative than to take my letter requesting the salvarsan to Dr. Scherr.

Late that afternoon Hsu Sir decided I should be taken back to the mission lest he have all the foreign devils down his neck.

In the weeks ahead I got to know Hsu Sir's wife, Hsu Tai, and wondered how a cultured, well-brought-up young woman could have become involved with these bandits. Although she never turned a hand to help herself as there was always a slave girl there, she was treated as a slave, too. When I knew her better, I asked her about her home.

She told me she was originally from Honan. Her people were well-to-do farmers. When she was fourteen Hsu had climbed in her window to loot her home and it was love at first sight. I guess they deserved each other.

A week went by. Finally the messenger returned with the ampoules and a letter from the dear doctor who insisted I must be a little foolish to hope that my patient could deliver a living child in her condition. I started the treatments anyway, staying close by to see there were no after-effects. After three very diluted treatments, Hsu Tai insisted she was feeling much better. No more guards came over my walls and the villagers no longer were bothered by raiders. The missionary at the church was most pleased that the raids had finally ceased.

"Does the man know the course of treatments will take eighteen months to two years?" he asked.

"No, Father, that is a small detail I omitted. I was most anxious to be away from their fort before I became a victim!"

Despite my fears, everything went well. During November I delivered a small son to the Hsu household. All things considered, the mother and baby were probably as healthy as they would ever be. Hsu Tai believed that all good things came in bunches: not only did she have a son but the Governor of Shantung had notified Hsu that he was to be made the deputy governor of the counties north of the Yellow River. Hsu's ego ran away with him.

There was to be a big state banquet and ceremony in Tsinan, at which Hsu Sir and his retinue, usually four bodyguards, were to be present. The bandit couldn't wait to get his grubby hands into the pockets of the taxpayers. Everything went well, or so the story goes. Then Hsu was shot through the head from behind. He was dead as a mackerel at the hands of one of his own guards.

In 1935 the Yellow River ran amuck inundating thousands of acres of farmland and causing great havoc in the southern areas. A call went out for medical personnel from missions to work with the International Famine Relief and the League of Nations Epidemiological units. Refugees were everywhere. I asked to be relieved of my job in Kuotown, and was returned to Tsinan.

There was talk everywhere about the changes that were taking place. The cry of "Fight Japan" was beginning to get louder, and "*Yang kuil tse*" (go home) became a daily greeting for people of the West. The Red Army had made its Long March and was settled in the special region, sort of a concentration camp authorized by the national government. Han Foo Chu issued such stupid decrees that they became jokes. He was ready to kill all the Reds and students in China.

But the warlords in China were helpless to stop events. It was as if the giant was awakening from sleep. The colourful young marshal, Chang Hsueh Liang, son of the Manchurian warlord, Chang Tse Liu, had become a figure to be recognized as the instigator of the movement for unity.

One fine September day in 1936 in Nanking, the young marshal kidnapped the General Chiang Kai-shek from under the noses of the heavy security that surrounded him and whisked him off by air to Sian, Sherise, and from there to the security of Lin Tung Villa some ten miles from Sian.

The whole country held its breath at the news of this terrible and magnificent act. It seemed as though all the young and progressive people were represented by the deed. All insisted the time had come for unity of all political parties and groups in China to fight the aggression of Japanese imperialism, preventing the subjugation of large areas of the country and the plundering of resources by this foreign power. Rumours were rampant that the general had been killed and that the Red Army occupied Sian.

Chiang Kai-shek refused to sign any agreements with the Communists or to make a United Front. The young marshal insisted that he indeed meant to kill the general in the event of his failure to sign. Finally, Madame Chiang and Mr. Donald (Madame's adviser) rushed to Lin Tung to counsel him. Up to this time, no one took the young marshal's threat seriously. One night the general attempted to escape in his nightshirt, and the sentries fired their guns at him. The bullet holes can still be seen in the wall of the house where he was held.

After much pleading and counselling from Donald and Madame Chiang he finally signed the articles of the United Front. The whole country went wild with joy. When the news came through in late evening, I went out to join the celebrating crowds.

The next days brought the details. The Communist delegates came down from Yenan, headed by Chou En-lai, who was one of the signatories of the historic articles. On October 10, 1936, it was all over. The general was back in Nanking where he made the young marshal a prisoner and banished him to an estate in Hunan. But the old man could not back out of the agreement. A new world was being born, the attitude of people changed, the Red Army became the Eighth Route Army. Chou En-lai was assigned to the Ministry of War, and the machine of confrontation began to take shape. Even if the central government and the reactionaries in the government had any ideas of blocking the United Front, they were powerless. The pressure from the whole community was like a giant sledge hammer. Confrontation with Japan was no longer a matter of lost resources; it was a matter of nationalist pride.

An incident happened to me while I was out for a walk on the city wall. Hundreds of students were drilling and marching until the old wall shook. A young student rushed up to me, shaking his fist in my face saying, "*Yang kuil tse*" (go home).

I said to him, "I don't want to go home. I want to go join the Eighth Route Army."

He looked scornful and said, "Do you know what the Red Army would do to you? They would kill you."

"Oh, I don't think so," I assured him. I did not know that a little more than a year later I would meet this young man on the streets of Yenan.

In June of 1937 we decided to return to Canada. I was not sure then whether or not I would ever be back. I had learned a great deal—a college education that couldn't be found in books. I had acquired a new language, a new way of life, fought with many doubts and hardships. As the holy man at Chu Li Chang had said, everything today is a preparation for another time.

CHAPTER FOUR

When I arrived home in Toronto I had no trouble getting a job at St. Joseph's Hospital in Sunnyside. I was assigned to a medical-surgical floor. Medical cases included everything from paraplegics to gout to geriatrics. Wages were still low but somehow we always managed a laugh, mostly at our own expense. But something new was added–an eight-hour day was being tried. While we had an eight hour day, the forty-hour week was a long way off. We worked six days a week for sixty dollars a month.

One afternoon, while talking to patients, an old man presented me with an article from the *Manchester Guardian* written by Agnes Smedley. In it she described the horror of civilian bombing and extreme distress and suffering of the Chinese people. No one knew I had been to China but this old man was a bit of a socialist and we used to talk about things once in a while. I used to call him a bloody old Red, which made him chuckle.

Later at our apartment, my sister Isobel gave me a mimeographed letter from Agnes Smedley, appealing for doctors and nurses for China. At the supper table the same evening Isobel chirped, "Sam Carr at Communist Party Headquarters wants to see you tomorrow at two o'clock." Next day was my day off, and I was reluctant to spend it meeting Sam.

After much argument with myself, I decided to go to the Party headquarters on King Street in Toronto. I felt a little out of place there. It was obvious that no one knew me.

As I knocked on the door, Sam's large voice shouted, "Come in and sit down!" There behind a great desk sat Sam in all his corpulence. After a bit of chit-chat about how I was doing and how I had been, he said, "We want you to go to China with Dr. Norman Bethune and an American, Dr. Fraad."

"You mean the Communist Party is sending us?" I asked.

"Who else?" he shouted.

He explained that Dr. Bethune had just come back from Spain where he had organized the Canadian Blood Transfusion Service and the blood banks. He spoke of the doctor with such enthusiasm I felt that Dr. Bethune must indeed be one of the saints–a member of the party echelon at least. I had heard much about the doctor before, most of it not good. I asked how I fit into the scheme of things, and was told I could speak Chinese and I knew the country.

"I want you to look after the doctor." Sam thumped his big fist on the desk.

I was speechless until I had gathered my wits. "But he is a big boy now and may not want anyone to look after him," I said, finally.

"What do you make at the hospital?" Sam asked.

"Sixty dollars a month," I replied.

"Big deal!" he exclaimed, adding something about nurses being a dime a dozen.

I knew my special attribute was my China experience. I had no intentions of being married or marooned on a hospital floor–those thoughts were appalling. I called Sam the next day and accepted the proposition.

Sam explained that first I had to go to New York to be screened by the newly formed China Aid Council. This organization was providing all the supplies and money the unit would need. The shipping of these supplies also came under their control.

In New York I met Dr. Bethune along with other members of the council at the home of the League for Peace and Democracy. Dr. Fraad did not join the unit for reasons I never learned. Another, Dr. Parsons, joined at the last minute.

In New York I was interviewed by Dr. Segal, a psychologist who scrutinized my motives for going on this mission. I had never met a member of this department of medicine before. I felt it might be fun to confuse him a little more than he could confuse me. He asked all kinds of questions about my family, including how I felt about my father. I flippantly assured him that I had only a nodding acquaintance with him. He insisted that he only wanted to know what kind of person I was, since this was a serious mission. Did I understand that the unit would be taken care of by the benevolence of the China Aid Council? He must have known all that I knew about China: the language, the living conditions. I wondered if he knew how damned silly he sounded.

I left New York the next day, not very impressed with the China Aid Council.

I did not see Dr. Bethune again until I reached Vancouver, a few days after New Year's Day. On January 8, 1938, I was piped aboard the *Empress of Japan* by a fellow Scotsman, Jimmy Mitchell, in full Highland dress. As I came aboard I noticed Dr. Bethune and Dr. Parsons leaning on the rail. I shook hands with them and Dr. Bethune asked, "Who the hell is the oatmeal savage piping, anyway?"

"Me, of course," I answered.

He gave me a contemptuous sneer saying, "I don't believe it! Tom's daughter a Scottish Nationalist."

I assured him I didn't care what he believed.

Our departure had been kept a big dark secret. The policy of the Government of Canada at that time was non-interventionist although it was selling vast amounts of planes, munitions, and scrap iron to Japan. Non-intervention simply meant that any country could invade another without fear of reprimand or sanctions or boycott from the so-called great powers (the United States, Great Britain, France, and Russia).

The passenger list on the *Empress* consisted mostly of missionaries returning to China, American army wives bound for Manila, and a few businessmen. There were also a dozen or so young American men booked for Hong Kong. No one seemed to care that they were mercenaries headed for the Chinese Air Force.

46

The crossing was rough. The wintry seas tossed the *Empress* around like a cork. Many times I was the only passenger in the dining room.

"How come?" I asked Captain Smith.

"You have webbed feet, I suppose," was his answer.

During most of the voyage we saw very little of Dr. Parsons and when he did put in an appearance he was usually inebriated. Dr. Parsons was a peculiar sort of person. His claim to fame was having served with the Grenfell Mission in Labrador.

When we reached Yokohama some twenty days later, both doctors went out to see the town, and later Tokyo, but they didn't go together. Japanese Customs and Immigrations officials carefully scrutinized the passports of those going ashore. Yokohama still smelled of rotten fish and sewage so I stayed on board.

Dr. Bethune returned quite early but Dr. Parsons just made it and was drunk as usual. They got into an argument and Dr. Bethune came to my cabin hopping mad. He insisted that we send a wire to the China Aid Council demanding that Parsons be recalled. I refused to go along with it.

A dreary sight met us when we reached Shanghai. Wusung was choked with soldiers and the river was glutted with every type of Japanese navy craft. Shanghai's waterfront harboured many Italian and German merchant ships. The grey diplomats of Britain, France, and the United States rode at anchor, unmuzzled guns gleaming and pointing shoreward, an evident display of might. Japanese soldiers drilled and camped on the river bank all the way to the international settlement. Hawkers or quarrelling rickshaw men were nowhere in sight.

Since I did not go ashore, my friends came out to the ship. We spent the day talking about the war, the tremendous changes it had brought, and the cruel suffering it had inflicted upon ordinary people, workers, and small businessmen. My friends felt that things would soon be back to normal and it would be business as usual. They thought the end of Chinese resistance was a certainty for the Chinese did not have that kind of endurance.

When we finally said our goodbyes I felt these friends

belonged in another world. It was perhaps a good thing that they did not know that they would never run their businesses as usual again. I advised them to go to the States and buy themselves a house so they would not be homeless. They thought I was nuts. The Japanese had never bothered foreign businesses before and everything would be okay. I was struck with a great sadness as we left Shanghai. People couldn't see beyond their noses.

Another day or so and we made the free port of Hong Kong, where there was no passport inspection. Within forty-eight hours one had to report to the police. Dr. Bethune was sure that we would be long gone in that time. Dr. Parsons was a little more cautious. He now launched his bombshell. He told us that contact had not been made with the persons who were to help us get to Hankow and there was no money left for hotel rooms. He had spent it on booze. He proposed that we go to the Sylvia Hotel where we could get space in the servants' quarters. The hotel was owned by a friend of his. This proved expensive because the hotel was located on the other side of Kowloon, and bus and car fare had to be squandered. Dr. Bethune was furious. I had not seen such a temper before, except in my father. He stomped and kicked everything in sight except Parsons. He sent a wire to New York and this time I signed it.

I suggested that we wire Agnes Smedley in care of the American Embassy in Hankow. Certainly someone there must know her or know where to find her. Both doctors were sure I had taken leave of my senses. What did I think a woman like Agnes Smedley would want with friends at the American Embassy?

I took it upon myself to send her a wire. In less than two hours she replied that we were booked on a CNA flight in two days. At last we were on our way.

The China Nation Airways flight was a bit late because of an air raid in Hankow. At Kai Tak airport, there was an assortment of Red Cross personnel, government officials, and missionaries all going into China. Dr. Parsons left our equipment in the freight sheds of the Canadian Pacific steamship company. Once on our way, the German pilot flew fairly low all the way to avoid being buzzed by Japanese planes.

Only the week before he had an encounter with Japanese fighter planes that left him with a few bullet holes in the plane's tail.

More than two hours later we landed on the south bank of the Yangtze at the Wuchang airstrip. Almost as soon as we hit the ground, crews of men started pulling camouflage nets over the aircraft. When I came down the ramp I noticed a man and a woman anxiously watching.

"Are there two doctors and a big fat nurse on this plane?" the lady asked me.

"I am the big fat nurse," I replied, assuring her that the two doctors would be down shortly.

"Well, I would hardly call you fat!" she said, joyfully adding that she was indeed glad to see us. This was Agnes Smedley and the man with her was a young reporter, Jack Beldon.

The driver of an ancient vehicle collected our baggage and requested that we get seated so he could get out of the airport area. When we were all seated, the old bus wouldn't move. The load was too heavy, so everything was transferred to rickshaws. Then away we went to the ferries, all of us except Dr. Bethune, who considered it below his dignity to be hauled around by another man. We arrived in good time. The ferry was on our side of the river and could not move till the all-clear sounded. Living under war conditions was a new experience for Dr. Parsons and myself. All traffic and pedestrians stopped when the urgent signals sounded.

As we waited we were jostled and shouted at by the rickshaw men and beggars fighting with each other to panhandle a few *cash*. The kids were most persistent, following right beside the cart crying piteously, "No got momma, no got poppa, not got whiskey soda." Their remarks about us were something else. I did not say anything until they got a little closer to me. One very offensive little man wanted to relieve me of my handbag. This ended in a short and profane altercation before he backed off. Agnes said she was sorry her vocabulary did not encompass swearing, although she often wished it did. I was astonished that her Chinese wasn't better. She couldn't go anywhere without her interpreter.

The Yangtze Kiang at Hankow is very wide, and Hankow

is considered a port city, for ocean-going vessels navigate the Kiang for 1,500 miles all the way to Chungking in West China. The ferries are large diesel-powered giants not unlike those that ply the Great Lakes in Canada. They carry cars, buses, ambulances, people, luggage, livestock, and garden produce. When they landed, livestock and produce went off first, then people.

The day had quite a wintry bite and we were glad to reach our destination, the Anglican mission where the diocesan bishop lived. Many people of all nationalities gathered at the mission house. You might find writers, doctors, embassy officials, air men, teachers, and missionaries, and not all of the Anglican persuasion. We enjoyed the warm hospitality of the venerable and wise bishop. The house was known as the *Yenan* (heaven axis) for the Eighth Route Army personnel were often found there having tea while discussing some subject of interest, important to the times. We arrived at the mission at tea time.

There were only five of us at the table. Conversation went from China to Spain to Britain to America and then back to Hankow. Dr. Bethune proved to be a good conversationalist. Agnes Smedley held her own also. I felt sorry for Dr. Parsons who had little to say beyond his profession. He was not a political person at all. He would make wild statements, which often sounded naive and brought contempt from Dr. Bethune.

Agnes Smedley was gifted with a spontaneous biting humour. She wore her hair in an atrocious style, as though she had turned a soup bowl over her head and whacked the hair off around it. She was really a liberated woman and probably one of the original proponents of women's rights. For all her joking and laughter it did not take her long to discover that Dr. Bethune did not appreciate an opinionated woman.

We had come to Hankow to make ourselves available to the Chinese government. However, the government had recently been moved to Chungking. The few government agencies left in Hankow included Chinese Red Cross personnel and some members of the Army Medical Service.

Dr. Bethune is welcomed by students at Kong Ta, the anti-Japanese aggression school in Yenan.

This drum was part of a local "telegraph" system. The sound of the drums carried news from village to village.

These chunks of ice were cut from a frozen river. Later, they would be packed in straw and stored in a deep hole.

These boys, dressed up and standing on stilts, were part of the Chinese New Year's celebrations.

An archway in Peking.

These children were a few of the many refugees.

Rose (left) in her cart in Peking. The mule's name was Dusty, and she had a tendency to kick anyone she didn't like.

This wagon served as the local "school bus." Here it is taking a group of girls home at the end of the day.

Rose and Agnes, holding old-fashioned rifles. The exceptionally long barrels were supposed to make the bullets go farther.

The author on a shopping spree in Peking.

Hankow was expected to fall to the Japanese before the spring of 1938 and most of the foreign wives and children had been evacuated.

That evening, Chou En-lai and Chin Bo Ku came to greet the newcomers. Mr. Chou at that time was in the Ministry of War of the Chiang Kai-shek regime. Mr. Chin held the position of co-ordinator of medical services of the Eighth Route Army. Both men were fluent in English so that conversation included everyone. The Chinese government had just completed an urgent secret matter, the laying of mines in the lower reaches of the river below Hankow. But like all secrets in China everyone knew about it. However, the populace felt a little safer since Japanese gunboats were two days downriver. The mines might not stop the advance but they would slow it down.

Japanese planes bombed the cities during the day and on moonlit nights. Casualties, especially civilian, were heavy, and hospital personnel were unable to cope with the sick and wounded. Supplies of dressings and medicine were low most of the time. Trains and transport trucks moved only between raids, which meant they usually travelled at night. Cities and towns came alive after five in the afternoon when air activity was over. Japanese pilots were nine-to-five flyers, except when there was a moon.

Late that first day in Hankow found Agnes, the two doctors, and myself down at Dr. R. K. S. Lim's rooms at the Lutheran mission home. Dr. Lim explained that his righthand man, Dr. Richard Liu, had not yet returned from a conference with the heads of the Army Medical Service. Dr. Lim wanted Dr. Liu to participate in whatever talks concerned us, since we had come to China to work for the central government. When he came, things started moving. Dr. Liu felt that our place was not with Army Medical Service but rather with a Red Cross unit. Dr. Lim asked if we would be willing to go to the Eighth Route Army. The articles of the United Front agreement stipulated that he was obliged to send medical units into the Communist regions. Dr. Lim, as head of the Chinese Red Cross, had big plans for his organization. He wanted a co-ordinated system of hospitals with an ambulance corps to transport the seriously wounded to the rear hospitals. His work was very different from his former lucrative position as head of the Physiology Department at Peking Union Medical College. His Red Cross position paid him two hundred Chinese dollars a month, called *mex* dollars on the world money market. Most of his doctors and nurses were afraid to go to the special area.

Dr. Bethune declared he would be delighted to go and that he hadn't ever had any intention of going anywhere else.

Dr. Bethune had a habit of telling people exactly what he wanted them to know and nothing more. He turned to me and asked if I would go with him. I said sure and with that the American-Canadian unit was ended. Dr. Parsons would have none of our plans. It took some persuasion to get him even to consider giving us the supplies the American Committee had provided for the unit. Finally after a lot of stomping, shouting, and foul language, he consented to hand over the cheques to Dr. Lim so that the supplies could be released. We had no idea how long it would be before the Red Cross could get the supplies to us. Communications at this point were impossible. Rail and road links with Hong Kong were severed in a few places. Chou En-lai dropped into the meeting later to welcome us to the Eighth Route Army Medical Service. He said he could not offer us anything but hard work and Dr. Bethune could expect nothing but a host of grateful patients. So ended our first day in China.

Dr. Lim insisted that we go out to the civilian hospitals while waiting to go north–they might even put us to work. He thought it might be a good idea if we met the Red Cross unit to which we would be attached. The unit was to have an obstetrical department, too. Everybody laughed at the idea of sending a baby team to an army base. We learned that the Eighth Route Army looked after all facets of medicine and education for civilians in their areas. Every child went to school, as did older people who were illiterate and wanted to learn. Crèches were connected with schools so that mothers, wives, and grandmothers could work in the co-ops and fields if they wished.

During the next week Dr. Bethune and I went out to the

Presbyterian mission hospital at Hanyang, another part of this Yangtze city of three cities. The hospital was grossly understaffed. The Chinese doctors and nurses did not wish to stay when their families were obliged to move to safer parts of the country. There wasn't much time for introductions after we arrived, so we just got to work. The waiting rooms were crowded with wounded from the last air raid. Halls were packed with homemade stretchers; some patients died before aid could be given them. The floors were sticky with blood and emesis and excrement. Two little ones were screaming in shock beside their dead parents. Legs, hands, and fingers were amputated; shrapnel picked out of wounds; bleeding stopped. The smell of blood is not a pleasant odour; it gets into your nose and it is hard to get rid of, especially during meals. At the time we didn't notice it much, for the work was urgent and fast or life trickled quickly away.

The operating room was staffed by Dr. Campbell and one helper, a Scottish nurse. They both worked on the wards as well when surgery was done. Relatives who came with a patient were allowed to stay and help look after him. The only accommodation for sleeping was the floor of the ward.

A surprise awaited us when we returned to the bishop's house, in the person of his beautiful daughter, Frances. She headed a delegation of young foreigners that had gone to Peng Teh Hwai's division to bring comfort and greetings to the Eighth Route Army soldiers in south Shansi. They had taken a very large shipment of socks, toothbrushes, soap, clothing, games, tobacco, and hospital supplies supplemented with a large cash donation. These gifts were collected and donated by sympathetic church groups and foreigners for the northwest partisans.

During the Chinese New Year, the Japanese planes ruthlessly bombed the cities day and night. The weather was damp and cold, which was no help to homeless people. Every shed and shelter, no matter how old, was occupied by refugees. The mission had a soup kitchen in the school in the daytime and bedded down nearly a hundred people every night. The sirens were going all the time it seemed.

During one of the few clear times I decided that I would

have my hair cut before going to Shansi. I went to a beauty shop on the San Tiao Gai. The hair stylist thought I was out of my mind to have my long hair cut. Short hair wasn't the latest Paris style.

A boyish bob was well under way when the darned siren screamed again. The barber, a White Russian, was firm. He pushed me gently out the door and told me to come back when the all clear sounded. Outside I found myself in a great crowd of hysterical, panic-stricken people with their belongings, animals, and children, all heading for the British concession. There, at least, was comparative safety, for the Japanese hadn't yet dared to bomb British property.

I made my way back to the house as quickly as I could only to find that the gates were locked and the doors and windows shuttered. The number one boy let me in with profuse apologies. After a few moments of sickly silence the anti-aircraft guns opened up, but they missed the nine Japanese bombers on their mission of death. The loud thud of bombs was discernible in the east and southeast of the city where troops were said to be concentrated. The raid lasted about two hours but it seemed more like a thousand years. Surely all the troops must have been wiped out.

On my way up to my room I met Agnes on the stairs. She greeted me with, "Great Scott you look a mess!" She very kindly finished my hair quite professionally and I still owe that barber for butchering my hair.

Later I went down to the parlour to see Chou En-lai and his wife, Cheng yin Chow, who had come to visit. Mr. Chou was under the impression that Canada was a wild bush country inhabited by Indians, a sprinkling of Frenchmen, and the Dionne quintuplets. Husband and wife made a comment about us in Chinese, which I picked up and responded to, shocking them a little. When they found I was fluent in Chinese they did not speak English to me anymore. Mr. Chou was a very dashing fellow even by western standards. His charisma, combined with the fact that he was multilingual, put him at ease in any company. He was usually the centre of the gathering. His eyes were usually very soft and enquiring with an amused twinkle but they could also be very severe.

In the interval between raids and calls from the hospital, Dr. Bethune and I were frantically collecting surgical equipment and medical supplies to last at least three months. February was nearly over before we were ready to go.

CHAPTER FIVE

One frosty cold morning we climbed aboard an Eighth Route Army truck, which took us from the mission house to the railway station. Before five in the morning we roared through the empty streets. Our freight was put in charge of a young man who wore an Eighth Route Army uniform under a Japanese greatcoat. His name was Chu and I felt he was not very pleased to have two foreigners who he thought could not speak to him. He was delighted when he found me arguing with a station guard.

That morning the Blue Express moved out on time. At five we were on our way–what fortune or misfortune lay ahead of us was most surely in the hands of the gods. Third class on any train is not designed for comfort but Chinese third class in those days and under war conditions was next to impossible. Above us, every kind of bag, basket, and suitcase was stuffed to the top of the car. Below us and in the aisle it was just the same. The seats were made of the hardest wood that could be found. The passengers were a conglomeration of soldiers, businessmen, farmers, women, and many children, most of whom were refugees going out of Hankow.

At noon it started to get hot. Along the route of the train, paddy fields were being cultivated. Women, knee deep in muddy water, planted tender shoots of rice. Fields of water were being ploughed by lumbering water buffalo pulling wooden, iron-tipped cultivators. The implement was so clumsy that a man had a difficult time holding it straight and upright.

The journey to Chengchow was not unlike others I had taken during my years in China. The peaceful tranquillity of the rural areas made war seem far away. Darkness had fallen when the train pulled into the station at Chengchow. We were now in Honan province.

As soon as the locomotive stopped, Comrade Chu opened a window and started pitching our belongings out on the platform. Dr. Bethune protested but Comrade Chu said if we waited till the passengers got off it would take all night. The Chinese are not squeamish about pushing or pulling to get where they want to go, a fact we found out many times before the next few days were over.

The Lunghai train was ready to leave for Sian but it was impossible for another passenger to get on. This was the connection we were to have made, so it was irritating to watch the train fade into the distance.

Accommodation for the night became our most urgent problem. Comrade Chu went into the city but soon came back to say that there were no rooms to be had at the inns or hotels. The station house was locked so the three of us, bag and baggage, stayed in a freight shed at the other end of the platform. The glass from the windows was long gone so the wind blew in one side and out the other. Comrade Chu dug down in his haversack and produced a candle. We unrolled our bedding on the floor.

A young woman with a baby in her arms came in out of the cold. Did I mind if she stayed? The place didn't belong to me so I said be my guest. She sat down on the floor shivering and was quite astonished when I handed her one of my quilts. At first she refused, protesting that she was warm enough and the cover would get soiled. Dr. Bethune insisted that she get some rest because she looked very tired. I explained to her that this man was a doctor who had just come to China to work. Her baby was five months old with matchstick arms and legs and a huge belly. His everlasting hunger caused him to cry a great deal and he looked like a little old man. Dr. Bethune excavated a can of milk along with a spoon and a cup from the bottom of one of the sacks. Comrade Chu was dispatched for a kettle of boiling water. Between them, the mother and Dr. Bethune spoonfed the baby a whole cup of milk.

"Keep your fingers crossed that he is satisfied and doesn't get indigestion and cry all night," said the doctor. We heard no more from him until daylight. His mother thanked the doctor profusely, saying that he had not slept so well for many nights. Dr. Bethune just grinned from ear to ear. Our visitor, confused and apprehensive, was afraid of what the new day might bring. The Chiang government provided nothing in the way of hostel facilities. The refugees were abandoned by them. The only assistance for the sick and wounded civilians was provided by the mission establishments and every church compound was bursting at the seams.

At the crack of dawn Comrade Chu came in with hot water for washing faces, then hot tea, steamed rice, and meat rolls. During breakfast I related the lady's story of her soldier husband and how no allowances or allotments were made to families. Dr. Bethune was appalled at the dereliction of duty by the government. He gave the lady a few dollars, which she reluctantly accepted after much *Ke che* (polite refusals). Her eyes were brimming with tears and she was humiliated, never having accepted charity before. Dr. Bethune assured her that it was not charity but a loan and that when the war was over he would be back for it.

At long last the Lunghai train came into the station. After a short wait it began the return trip to Sian. Dr. Bethune bullied the conductor into exchanging our third-class tickets for *wagon-lits* (second-class compartments). It cost him twenty-five dollars. The warm, comfortable compartment was a far cry from the jumbled togetherness of a third-class carriage or the freight sheds.

The closer we got to Tungkuan the higher and more bare were the yellow loess cliffs. Some were terraced with amazing symmetry, both man-made and natural. There were no trees and very few shrubs and bushes on the bare surface. Tungkuan city was some distance from the station and siding. The city walls towered up in front of us like those of a forbidding mediaeval fortress. At the city's south gate a sentry asked to see our passes. Whether he could read or not we did not enquire but after they were examined, he handed them back to Comrade Chu, saluted, and we were on our way to the Eighth Route Army barracks.

I guess all army barracks are the same. Every soldier in the place was busy. The commanding officer had no private office; only a corner of the common room, which also served as a dining room, reading room, and medical clinic when necessary. The long rooms were bare, the walls whitewashed, and the only decoration was three pictures–Chiang Kai-shek, Mao Tse-tung, and Lenin. The floor was hardpacked earth and there were two rows of long tables down the centre with benches to sit on.

After a wash, some food, and a little rest, we were allowed to inspect the compound. A dozen soldiers were busy in the courtyard cleaning guns while sunning themselves.

Dr. Bethune looked after some wounded who had come in the day before. They did not have a doctor at the barracks, only a dresser, but he knew his business. Removing bullets from thighs and shoulders and setting broken bones was to be the routine for the next few weeks. With me nearby as interpreter and nurse, Dr. Bethune operated in old huts, barns, or any shelter near at hand. On one occasion, the officer in charge asked whether Dr. Bethune would see a civilian patient for him, as a favour. The man had been wounded some time ago and the leg was still infected. After seeing the patient Dr. Bethune decided that the gangrenous leg had to come off or the man would die. After much discussion with the family and the officer it was agreed that the operation should be done at once. There was only one gas lamp in town (one of Coleman's antiques) so it was commandeered. In the barracks room, Dr. Bethune and the local Chinese doctors (naturopaths) amputated the limb above the knee. Dr. Bethune gave them minute instructions for post-operative care as we would probably be long gone before the sutures were removed.

I was cleaning up after the operation when a very aggressive woman with bound feet hobbled in to demand the leg. Despite her bound feet she was quite tall and used to very hard work as her black trousers and jacket attested to. She demanded his leg! What for? She went into great detail. How could a man present himself in the next world with only a leg and a half? Dr. Bethune came back to see what all the argument was about. When I told him, he said, "Oh come on, this is the twentieth century." He could not believe that people were so steeped in superstition. He told me very definitely that the woman couldn't have the maggoty leg, but she got it anyway and took it home to bury until the old boy died. Then it would be buried with him.

Dr. Bethune took this opportunity to have a little talk on just what he expected of me. I was never to call him by his first name, a sin I had not yet committed. Ours was to be a doctor-nurse relationship. Otherwise we were to have no particular contact. I told him not to worry. It could be no other way in professional work. Then, too, I was not to take it upon myself to diagnose or treat patients. He knew I had not but he was just telling me. I wondered what brought that on and I was hopping mad. I was a servant, no more, no less. I did not show my anger, at least I hoped I didn't. I resolved to put forth every effort to please the good doctor.

Preparing to cross the Yellow River presented some problems because the river had been in flood for some weeks. Large chunks of ice floated in the water, and the banks near the dikes were knee deep in mud and water. Comrade Chu insisted that we accompany a boatload of soldiers and pack animals.

When we reached the Shansi side, each soldier took off his shoes (cloth or straw sandals), rolled his trousers above his knees, and waded through the mud. The boatman said he would carry me across the mud for a dollar but I waded because the others were wading. The water was freezing. Halfway through the quagmire I was not sure if I had feet anymore and my temples ached, but I was determined not to be a slowpoke.

We then walked with our baggage to the Fenglintu station about a mile away. The small wooden train was jammed with passengers, and the aisles crammed with innumerable bags, baskets, boxes, and bundles. Babies and small children were howling in protest at being shoved around. Their tired, irritated mothers would plead, scold, and soothe them with sweets in an effort to keep them quiet. No matter how recalcitrant a child was, a Chinese mother never lifted her hand to him.

Comrade Chu suggested that we liberate, commandeer, or just plain occupy a quiet, empty box car he had noticed on the end of the train. We carried our bundles, boxes, and baskets to the end of the train and took possession without interference. At the end of the box car stood two bales of hay, which Comrade Chu immediately spread over the floor. Bedding rolls were unpacked and mine was pushed behind some boxes to give me a little more privacy.

Comrade Chu disappeared for a while returning with a double-decker orange crate and a wash basin. A gasoline can that had been left behind was soon filled with fresh water. Out of nowhere, he produced a cake of Lux soap with some very colourful Japanese terry towels. (Lever Brothers had a tremendous soap factory in China.) Presently three young women teachers came to occupy the car, protesting that they had been there first and left only to pick up their gear.

"Well, be our guests," urged Comrade Chu who stipulated that the only restriction was against people who snored. The girls then moved in, insisting that a large flannellette sheet be hung to close off our quarters. The girls were strictly new China–with bobbed hair, unbound feet, and army uniforms. They were going to the new Academy of National Resistance in Wutai Shan. After that they would be cadres and teachers in the small communities in occupied territories.

Several hours after the scheduled time the train was under way. For amusement Dr. Bethune entertained us with his ukulele and sang Spanish songs. The girls had a Chinese violin and a flute, which they played. And they sang war songs of the partisans of north China. I learned the words quite easily but to put the words to the catchy tunes so they sounded right was another matter. Comrade Chu listened to all this, then politely asked us if he could have a turn. He took a neat little package out of his pocket containing his most prized possession, a mouth organ. Comrade Chu was no amateur. His repertoire was extensive, even including some songs with an American flavour, and some revealing a

Russian influence. When he finished by playing "Yankee Doodle" we clapped loud and long.

We all recognized that Chu was a remarkable fellow. Nothing seemed to upset his equilibrium. He could prepare meals when no food was around. Opening up one of the boxes he would produce a pot, some rice, and the equipment to cook it on–an ageing, one-burner Coleman camp stove. Then, at every stop, he would disappear for awhile, returning with roast chickens, barbecued beef or pork, and *shansi lsiao bing* (a hard bread with crunchy crust covered with sesame seeds).

All our wagon lacked was electricity and plumbing, and I was fairly comfortable even though I had never travelled in a freight before. An outside observer, especially a westerner, might have raised his eyebrows at our bizarre company. The Japanese planes routed us out of our beds twice during the night and early morning, keeping us on needles and pins till we came to Linfen.

Forty-eight hours after we left Tungkuan, the old Tung Pu express pulled in at Linfen station. The town was completely evacuated of civilians. Only retreating soldiers could be seen on the streets. Dr. Bethune made his way to the China Inland Mission and found it empty, except for a caretaker. He returned to the station just as the sirens blew. Crew and passengers scrambled over barbed-wire fences and coal piles making for an open field. I picked a spot near a grave, a cone-shaped mound with an altar beside it, but it afforded little protection. The altar was loaded with food, wine, and money, probably offered by relatives so that the occupant of the grave might enjoy himself in eternity. I wasn't expecting anyone to be there, but it seemed I had the company of an old man, half sitting, half kneeling by the altar, his head resting on his arm, the other hand straight out. I paid no attention to him and he did not speak.

After the raid was over I said, "The raid is over, *Lo yeh*, better get up now!" No answer. Thinking that he hadn't heard me, I put my hand on his shoulder. Imagine my surprise and fright when I found he was dead. I fled with wings on my feet.

On returning to our deluxe wagon I found Comrade Chu all in a dither. Where had I been? He had been frantically looking for me because I was his medium of communication with Dr. Bethune. He had tried to tell Dr. Bethune with sign language that the Japanese troops were about ten miles away and advancing. The division headquarters at Hung Tung had moved. He did not know to where but he did know that we could not get there. A fine kettle of fish! To make things a little more exciting the train we had just gotten off was not returning to Tungkuan.

"How will we get back?" I asked Comrade Chu.

"Well, we can start walking back but not to Tungkuan, that is too far."

Up to now I had not said anything to Dr. Bethune about our predicament except that the Japanese were less than ten miles away. Dr. Bethune was feeling very frustrated because no one seemed to be making any move to look after the wounded. He was, I decided, a doctor first–concerned only with the person who might be sick or wounded. Certainly he wasn't overly concerned about our difficulties. I assumed that somewhere under this obsession there was a human being. Later I wondered even about this.

Comrade Chu disappeared again. This time he was gone for the better part of an hour. He returned with three husky Eighth Route Army soldiers to pick up our belongings for shipment on another freight train. When the quartermaster of the 124th Division looked at our passes, he said, "Of course you know that we have absolutely no accommodation. You will have to sleep on top of the rice sacks." I felt that the most important thing to us at that moment was not how we got going but to just get going.

I could not delay breaking the news to Dr. Bethune any longer. I knew he wouldn't like it and in all probability would hold me personally responsible for our fate. Sure enough, he damned me for everything he could think of. "Of all the damned inefficiency I have ever seen!" On he thundered in unprintable words. Even the quartermaster had no difficulty understanding the gist of the storm. "Where in hell are your brains?" the doctor wanted to know.

Our new quarters were not nearly as comfortable as those we had left at the box car of the Tung Pu line. Try sleeping on hundred-pound bags filled with rice and you'll soon discover that a quiet comfortable sleep is impossible. You change position every few minutes or muscles you never knew you had start screaming at you. Personally, I was so exhausted that the puff of the locomotive and the roll of the wheels brought relief and security and I soon fell asleep. We had not gone very far when the train stopped. We were soon to discover the reason. Outside, a good old-fashioned fight was going on, Chinese style. This was not a fight with fists, but good old yakkity-yak. I never saw two Chinese fight with their fists but they can sure use their tongues. I got down off the rice and went up front to see what all the noise was about. Apparently the engineer had abandoned the train, leaving the fireman alone to run it. I looked around to see where we were, and saw only three mud huts without doors and a station house of sorts.

Again it fell to me to break the news to Dr. Bethune who grunted, "I might have known." I had come to wish he had another interpreter.

Around six in the morning, the quartermaster's staff began scouting the area for water and wagons to haul the supplies away. The whistle stop we were marooned at was Goa Si. Although we had travelled a few miles, we were a long way from the Yellow River. We had to get there before the crossings were stopped and time was running out.

The Japanese airmen were out early every day, dropping bombs on any small village that might have a soldier quartered. We watched them from a distance, flying very low. Each time a bomb dropped, a wall of earth rose skyward with a thud, and houses and trees were no more. Their favourite game was strafing anything that moved, be it a dog, a child, or a soldier.

We watched with interest as trains passed through this empty place, refugees crowded uncomfortably together even on the roofs of the coaches and on the coal car of the engine. Unkempt, tired, frightened old men and women with children, all clutching their few precious possessions, fled into an unknown world.

One old man sat on top of his coat in the engine tender with his sole possession, a small wire-haired dog. Dr. Bethune was interested in him because of his great age and asked why he was going so far away. He shrugged his shoulders, saying, "*Mu yu fu*" (I have no luck). A Japanese bomb had hit his home and killed his family, including his immortality, his small grandson whom he loved very much.

"What are you going to do to make a living out there?" I asked him.

"What can I do now? I am old, my life is nearly over but I cannot stay to receive foreign soldiers," he lamented. As the old locomotive pulled the train away the old man looked wistfully down the track.

Eight trains passed through the deserted stop that day. By nightfall we were alone on the lonely rail siding again, with a dozen people or so, a trainload of rice, and three heads of battered green cabbage.

While the war went on and delayed our travel, Dr. Bethune and I accompanied by two *hsiao kuies* (little devils or young soldiers to be) went exploring the countryside.

To call the boys *hsiao kuie*, a term of endearment reserved for small children, is a hangover from the old Red Army days and the Long March. Some of the kids didn't know who their parents were or where they were since many had been killed. Many were children of indentured slaves. Quite a few of these fellows were no longer small and some were veterans of the Long March with the Red Army. One of these bigger little devils, now quite grown up and perhaps fifteen, came with us. He had buck teeth and carried a revolver. He was very tall with a heavy jaw and was quite pleasant in spite of his officious manner.

"Is your life in the Army better than when you were a slave?" I asked. He looked at me as though I had taken leave of my senses.

"That's a funny question–now I can read and write and I attended school!" He added that when the war was over he would go to school in Shanghai or Peking.

Dr. Bethune and I finally sat down under a mulberry tree just off the road near the entrance of a village. Dr. Bethune sat on one side of the trunk and I on the other, leaning against the tree, listening to the heavy silence. Suddenly a drop of fluid splotted on my hand–funny! I wiped it away. A while later another splat. I drew Dr. Bethune's attention to it. Both of us got up together to search the tree branches. When we moved away from the tree to see what might be hidden, we saw, head down in the uppermost branches, the small body of a child clad in red trousers. Dead for how long? How did it get there? "My God! My God!" whispered Dr. Bethune. A curse, a requiem, a prayer.

We hurried back to the train leaving the little one in its treetop grave. When we got there we found what seemed like dozens of wagons, and shouting, sweating men carrying rice sacks off the cars on the double. All the medical supplies went on two wagons.

Beside the station house several soldiers were waiting for Dr. Bethune to look after their wounds. He spent an hour with forceps, dressings, and sutures; their wounds were rotten. Comrade Chu said the men weren't from "our army" because the leaders of "our army" would not allow men to be neglected for so long. We were finding out a lot of things about "our army" on this trip.

Once we were underway, it became evident that our wagon was to become a mobile dressing vehicle. Dr. Bethune, like the good Samaritan, bound the wounds of all who came to him. The grapevine carried the news of our arrival ahead of us. Everyone with wounds or sores or ulcers stopped us. Sometimes the wagons would not wait for us and the aggravated quartermaster would shout at the doctor because he had to deliver us across the river as soon as possible. Looking after patients only held him up. Didn't we know that the Japanese Army was closing in? Dr. Bethune just laughed and said, "Never mind, we'll make it."

Our crew made quite a sight. My first thought was that we could be a wagon train on the Canadian prairies in the nineteenth century. Then I remembered that forty odd wagons stretched out on a dusty road made a wonderful target.

The third morning out was a bright sunny day though the sound of Japanese planes bothered us. We kept going but always looked for a possible shelter just in case! Here the land was as flat as a table top–not even a gully or a ditch to hide in.

Then it happened! Two Japanese planes spotted us. Nearly everyone moved quickly to the hollow archway of a pagoda beside the road. I could not see Dr. Bethune anywhere. My flight ended in a clump of castor beans. The horses and donkeys stampeded with fright.

The planes came down over the whole caravan and circled back again. They dropped their first bomb in the centre of the wagons, which flew apart like paper. The earth heaved a little as rice, dirt, and wood spewed skyward. It was my first experience of close war conditions and I don't mind saying that I was scared spitless. From the smelly cover of the castor plants, I could see the planes come round again, strafing.

I felt a little sick to my stomach. When things settled down, three mules in front of me fell heavily to the ground groaning with pain, blood streaming from their nostrils. The planes circled several times dropping more bombs and strafing. More wounded animals fell to the ground.

Several wounded men were screaming. A bomb landed near where I was lying, covering me with earth, spring wheat, and castor plants. When I finally scrambled out from under, I had two holes in my pant leg, but nary a scratch on me. I knew I had a charmed life, though I was shaking.

Four of the men were badly wounded. Six wagons and two drivers were not to be found. Only a big crater remained in the road where they had been. Kindly peasants from a nearby village carried the wounded to their homes where Dr. Bethune gave them emergency treatment and dressings. I could hardly function from fear. Dr. Bethune didn't get angry, but he pontificated: "Every man must have two baptisms in his life–once with water and once with fire. You have just had your baptism of fire."

"You are nothing but a bloody missionary," I said, without thinking.

Then, Dr. Bethune blew his fuses. He yelled and screamed, talking so quickly that I don't think he knew exactly what he was saying.

"Don't you ever say anything like that again, you dizzy bitch!"

By that time I could not stop crying, so I just left in the middle of a dressing. I encountered the quartermaster and Comrade Chu who were busy regrouping the wagons. They were determined to continue but only at night. The villagers urged us to leave the wounded with them but Comrade Chu wouldn't consider it. Stretchers were made for the two severely wounded drivers.

About dusk the *hsiao kuie* whom we'd nick-named Buck came to tell us we were ready to go. The driver had orders that under no circumstances was he to stop or allow Dr. Bethune to care for wounded. The night was cold and the thud of Japanese guns coming ever closer didn't help much. Before dawn a gentle rain began to fall. Along the road ahead of us, and on each side of us, was a trail of bobbing, moving lights, seeming endless in their continuity. As we came close to one lantern the peasant carrying it said he was leaving his village and moving to Shensi, for safety. He was guiding two donkeys who followed him like dogs, without a halter or leash. The first donkey had two enormous baskets attached to either side of a wooden saddle, which in no way hindered the animal's movement. They seemed to be stuffed with all the family's possessions. A small daughter slept in one basket, securely wrapped in blankets and quilts; while the other held a teapot, cups and bowls, and a protesting baby pig. On the very top, a small basket made of reeds housed half a dozen baby chicks. The peasant's wife was sitting side saddle on top quite comfortably. Cradled lovingly in her arms was the sleeping son and heir. The mother-in-law sat on the second donkey with a few of her precious things.

"We left nothing for the Japanese, not even water, for we filled the well with stones and rubbish," the farmer assured us. Dr. Bethune said he had never seen it fail. The landed rich and the merchants evacuated with their wealth; the poor, who had nothing to lose, stayed behind. I thought he was mistaken but said nothing.

CHAPTER SIX

It was not yet daylight when we reached the city of Kiang Chow. Somewhere in the murky darkness, church bells called the faithful to early mass. Buck and another soldier had gone ahead to find lodgings and keep an ear to the grapevine, for in old China the grapevine carried vital information as well as gossip. Buck was waiting for us at the edge of town. Another lad had stayed at the inn to have food prepared and to find a place for our wounded.

The sleepy old innkeeper, between yawns, told us he had prepared tea, hot bread, and meat in one of the back rooms. A solitary bean-oil lamp flickered on a roughly made black table. Somewhere at my feet a frightened rat scuttled for shelter. Dr. Bethune went into the next room to sleep. I just snoozed where I sat, my head on my arms on the table.

The local populace heard there was a doctor in town and about seventy-five people had gathered in different rooms in the inn waiting to be looked after. Buck gave them a detailed account with sound effects of the happenings of the last couple of days. Through my half-sleep I heard Dr. Bethune mumbling softly. Then he became louder till he shouted. He could stand the noise no longer. He came stalking out like a thunderstorm in long johns, picked Buck up by the collar, and deposited him outside the door, saying, "Now for Christ's sake, shut up!" The audience was flabbergasted, for the loss of face was unthinkable.

Buck, however, was unperturbed.

"Oh, Dr. Bai has a big temper *da pichi*, but he has a good heart and golden hands," said Buck very reverently.

Indeed, within an hour, we were both at work. Our wounded were dressed and comfortable and fed. Then Dr. Bethune started on the villagers. A young man in his early twenties came asking about his leg. Dr. Bethune suggested it might be better if he had a look so the young man took off the puttees and the covering he had on the wound. Yards of dirty rags came off exposing pulpy skin ulcers of tuberculosis, pus draining down his leg, and a most noxious odour.

I said, "Oh, tuberculosis." Swiftly, the great hand of discipline fell on me.

"I did not ask you to diagnose this case. Take him to one of the rooms in the inn and apply fomentations every hour."

Where the hell did Dr. Bethune think we were–in a Montreal hospital?

Armed with some spanking new Japanese terry towels taken from the quartermaster I applied the foments. I left the patient on a *kong* after instructing him not to move. I intended to come back within the hour. Shortly after, Dr. Bethune screamed my name at the top of his lungs. I rushed into the patient's room. The doctor turned a dark countenance on me.

"Don't you know how to do anything right?" he demanded. I looked at the foments in shock, for there before my eyes were the dirtiest, greasiest rags in the whole world. I found that the patient had taken off the new towels and sold them to the innkeeper for a few pennies so he could eat.

Dr. Bethune said that only a stupid youngster would consider that he would believe such a phoney story. I was furious but managed to hold back my angry tears as I went back to the dressing room. Then, a leper came in with his cane and cup. That was all I needed! Other patients were ignored until the leper had been cared for. Dr. Bethune asked many questions about his disease as he examined his suppurating fingers and toes. I offered no diagnosis this time and acted only as unofficial interpreter. I was the doctor's only contact with patients. My knowledge of Chinese had grown so that there wasn't much I could not say, understand, or read, and I could even write legibly. Sometimes Dr. Bethune refused to believe the substance of my translations. This was one of those times. The leper said he had been to many doctors and they all told him the same thing.

"You will put dressings on this man's hands and give him some vitamin pills," ordered Dr. Bethune.

"Sir," I said sarcastically, "I refuse to put dressings on this man's hands or to give him vitamin pills."

Whether the good doctor liked it or not I would have my say. First of all I pointed out that dressings on his hands would not solve his problem. Even he knew that he had leprosy. Vitamin pills had never, as far as I knew, cured the disease and I considered it a bit hypocritical of Bethune to play God. So I spoke my mind. I explained that lepers were cruelly isolated in this country; they were not allowed on the street except with a little clapper. They were obliged to wear white clothing, white being the colour of the dead. No store permitted them entrance; even dogs ran from them barking. I knew he did not believe me.

After that episode, the so-called clinic was closed for the day. I felt sorry that I had made such an issue of the incident. I felt that Dr. Bethune was a dedicated humanitarian but even dedicated people didn't have all the answers. He said nothing until after we had something to eat, then he suggested that I take a walk with him. I knew by the air of professional dignity he assumed that anger was about to explode.

"You are truculent, self-sufficient, overconfident and absolutely no use to me–and you are also a disgrace to your illustrious father," he fumed.

I agreed with him. "I always tried to be a disgrace to my father." The doctor had no right to sit in judgement on me and I told him so. At this point I felt I was just about the last person in creation who should have made this journey with him.

"I will be pleased to leave this bloody unit when we reach Sian," I told him.

When we returned to the inn, several soldiers were waiting

to have their wounds dressed. For some it was the first medical care they had had. Their clothes were dirty, ragged, and covered with lice and blood.

"Where are the other boxes of dressings and drugs?" Dr. Bethune wanted to know.

"We don't have any more dressings or salves or solutions and we have only a dozen vials of catgut, sir," I replied. The doctor looked for the boxes of dressings but they were gone long since. Most of the supplies and bandages had been used on the many hundreds of patients Dr. Bethune had treated in all the shanties, lean-tos, and ditches from Tungkuan to Kiang Chow. He refused to believe that they hadn't been hidden away in some corner.

Later in the evening three soldiers came looking for the doctor. How did they get so far from their own troops? They couldn't be sure how they got lost–they may have been AWOL. Their wounds were awful, and covered by pus-filled paper dressings. Dr. Bethune asked them if the armies didn't have doctors or dressers. The soldiers couldn't be sure as there were no hospitals near the front. We found ourselves in no-man's-land, in what is considered the front, ahead of an advancing Japanese Army and at the rear of a retreating Chinese Army.

After the evening meal we held a conference and decided to wait till morning before leaving. Two *hsiao kuies*, a mule skinner, and myself were all for moving now. The next morning the only way to cross the river was swim or be carried.

Dr. Bethune suggested that I be carried on a chair. I said no! I would swim across in my underwear.

"You can't do that, you'll scandalize the population," he admonished. Either way I had a gut feeling that I was going to get wet, but to stop the argument and against my better judgement I consented to being carried across.

Four men carried the chair. As we got halfway over I thought, so far so–and the next moment I was sitting in the water! One of the carriers had slipped and lost his balance. The first thing I saw when I stood up and got the water out of my eyes was Dr. Bethune, holding his belly and bent over laughing. I got up and walked away and refused to speak to Dr. Bethune for the next twenty-four hours.

Our next stop was a village where only one wealthy family lived. I was assigned to a room that had been the nuptial chamber of the bride. The occupant was no longer here but her lovely, ornately carved rosewood furniture and red silk wall hangings remained. The room looked a little forlorn but I could lock the door and be alone for awhile, and enjoy the luxury of a real bed, something I had not had for quite some time. I took a bath, put my hair up in pins and retired for the night, leaving my precious lipstick and cream out for the morning. During the night, a packrat came in and made off with my lipstick; in its place he left a piece of willow bark. Next morning before breakfast I toured the "shops" but I could find no lipstick. While out on the shopping tour I bought a large bowl of hot fermented rice with an egg poached in it. This is an old Shantung favourite of mine. On a cold morning it is just the thing to get you going.

Soon we were on the road again and each time we stopped it seemed to me we acquired more and more ragged, hungry, and unkempt children, who seemed to get younger all the time. The quartermaster kept the wagons on the move. Children, however, were not our only problem. The wounded besieged Dr. Bethune asking for care. The walking wounded and stretcher cases lacked sedation, food, conveyances, or money to get them to Shensi. Some of the soldiers hadn't been paid for many months. They existed on what they could scrounge or steal from the peasants.

We also encountered many wounded animals along the way, including a tailless mule with three broken legs. Dr. Bethune asked Buck for his gun.

"Sorry, good Dr. Bai can have anything he wants but not my gun," was the reply. The owner of the beast would demand payment, Buck explained. Dr. Bethune slashed the carotid artery with his own hunting knife and the hapless beast screamed, kicked his broken legs, then was quiet and out of his misery.

We carried on, the sun getting hotter and everybody getting grouchier. The quartermaster, Lao San, would not stop until we reached Gin Hsien. He looked with small favour upon the additional children who came to us for help.

"How can you turn a child away, Comrade quartermaster–is he not a citizen of tomorrow?" I asked him.

At Gin Hsien we were scheduled to spend the night with a poor family, where we found fleas, sand flies, and multitudes of other crawling beasties coming to life in the warm spring weather. The natives had never seen a big-nosed foreigner before so I was not surprised when an old lady came hobbling with a cane, smiling from ear to ear, to feel the skin on my face and hands and my hair, "ay-ya-ing" at the whiteness of my skin and the yellowness of my hair.

The quartermaster insisted that I must tell Dr. Bethune not to see any more patients for we were to move shortly. Japanese troops had occupied Kiang Chow, the town that we had left a few hours ago. Dr. Bethune took it upon himself to tell Lao San just where to go when I translated the message. I did not have to translate for Lao San as Dr. Bethune's meaning came through loud and clear.

Dr. Bethune was a gifted physician with a manner that gave patients confidence. At heart he was a missionary; he had a great love for humanity. The abandoned hungry children were so pitiful that the doctor often fed them himself. He went to the quartermaster to secure trousers and jackets for them. He argued that the Japanese didn't want Chinese uniforms and that we would most likely have to abandon them anyway.

One young lad adopted me, saying he had asked the quartermaster if he could have the job of being my *hsiao kuie*. Of course, he didn't know what to do with his two-year-old sister who was such a nuisance, he said, she couldn't even feed herself. He brought her to me to care for while he tended to the business of getting her some dinner. She was very cute although she had been badly neglected.

At last we were within sight of Hotsin and only two miles from the Yellow River. The adjutant had preceded us to find lodgings. After the children and the wounded were cared for and fed we started to walk to the river, accompanied by Buck.

A short distance from town we were stopped by sentries who demanded to see our passes. Two soldiers, covering us with fixed bayonets, asked, "Why do you foreigners want to leave Shansi? You have nothing to fear from the Japanese." How naïve. Our passes and baggage were approved for crossing the river but we would have to wait till morning.

The barge arrived from the Shensi side of the river in the grey hour before dawn. Soon animals, soldiers, children, and the big noses were loaded and headed for midstream. The crossing took nearly three hours because of the heavy load and the swift current, which carried us several miles downstream. The barge was towed back with heavy ropes and the chant "Aiyo, Haiyo" as the pullers kept time with their feet on the cold ground.

On the Shensi side, the Seventy-sixth Division of Provincial Troops was setting up machine-gun nests in the oddest places. Army medical units were preparing for action, boiling instruments, and getting splints, anaesthesia, and sedation ready. Adjutant Li led us to a small village nestled over the brow of a hill. We had left Comrade Chu in Shansi. He had to return to his unit.

The village where we put down our baggage was deserted except for a man and his wife who were too poor to leave. They had nothing to lose by staying as long as the Japanese were on the other side of the river. The lady of the house prepared food for us while her husband sat on the *kong* preparing to smoke his opium pipe.

I had never seen anyone smoke opium before so I was all eyes. The pipe was made of hollow bamboo rod about twelve inches long. About two inches from the heel or end of the stem was a round bowl fluted to a small opening in the top. Tweezers, a small pick, cotton balls, a bunsen burner, and a small round silver box containing black opium tar completed the kit. The old man rolled some cotton around the pick, dipped it into the tar, and heated it over the burner. When the tar got smoky he stuffed it into the opening on the top of the bowl. He held the pipe over the flame and drew up the smoke. Opium has a pungent smell and is an acquired taste. The smoker inhaled several long drags until a sensation of peace came over him. He didn't lose consciousness, only looked a little vague. All this time his wife raved at him about spending the family finances, but it fell on deaf ears. I took a drag on the pipe just for the heck of it. My stomach did a couple of flip-flops.

Dr. Bethune, Buck, and I walked to the river's edge to see how preparations were getting along and if there were any Japanese around. The whole Shensi bank and dikes were honeycombed with trenches, telephone wires, machine gun nests, piles of long belts of bullets for the machine guns, cannons and other machinery. High overhead we watched four spots come in from the north, and grow into the monsters they really were before passing over us. No matter how many air raids I went through, I could not stop the paralyzing fear that overtook me. I never got braver.

By early afternoon the Japanese soldiers and artillery came into view. We were trapped beside the river. They machine-gunned everything in sight, including two barges in midstream, loaded with old men, women and children. The screams of fright, pain, and terror echoed and re-echoed through the cold air. Blood reddened the black water of the river for just a moment, then became part of the blackness. A bullet whizzed past my ear. Buck decided it was time to take refuge in one of the trenches. We followed the trench to its end and crawled out onto the road.

We returned to our dwellings only to find the children, pots, pans, and everything gone. Adjutant Li came down the road and reprimanded us severely for running off. We might have been killed. Li added that the *hsiao kuies* would take us to our new quarters in some caves across a ravine. Some peasants who had migrated from Shantung during the 1936 floods and who had never been well enough off to return home had stayed and reclaimed a few acres of silt land along the watery banks of the river.

The six caves they had built were oblong, about twenty feet in length with a curved ceiling. The *kong* was hewn out of the earth at the end of the wall. In front of the cave stood a wooden wall with a paper window and door. We shared the cave with soldiers, children, the family, chickens, and an assortment of crawling critters.

During the early morning hours the weather turned very cold despite the twenty or thirty odd persons in the cave. The cold was accentuated by high winds. The gods were angry, the old ladies assured us. The young soldiers lit a fire under the *kong*, which awakened millions of bugs and fleas that had been dormant since the year one. We had three choices–freezing to death, choking to death on smoke, or being eaten alive by bugs. Personally I preferred the freezing–it was less painful. Dr. Bethune said the "mechanized units" that attacked him during the night were fierce as his arms were reddened and full of lumps.

Dr. Bethune could not tolerate the idleness thrust upon him by the necessity of staying in one place to wait for trucks to come from Sian. He was like a bear with a boil in his ear. How long we would have to wait for the vehicles was anyone's guess. Lao San had sent two soldiers to Sian to the Eighth Route Army headquarters to request trucks for us.

As time passed, Dr. Bethune became intensely grave, living within himself a great deal. Nothing pleased him and he scowled continually. Most of the time he was beyond the reach of conversation. You could say something to him and he wouldn't answer. He wasn't given to laughter but at every opportunity he made fun of me, my lipstick, my frivolities, my playing ball with the soldiers or *hsiao kuies*. By now I was sure I was the last person on earth who should have come with this man. He felt that there was something missing in my make-up.

Dr. Bethune firmly believed that Marxist doctrine alone imbued men with compassion, honesty, and a sense of duty. In his work with the sick and wounded he was a man dedicated to the service of all mankind. Besides being a healer, he was also a writer, an artist, and a scientist.

We were confined to our small area for four more days before the fighting stopped and we were able to have a fire outside. During the evenings we sat by an open fire. It was here that I heard about Dr. Bethune's wife, Frances, the light of his life. Although I had never met her I learned a great deal about her and how wonderful she was. Dr. Bethune blamed himself for the failure of their marriage. He was very unhappy in his personal life and couldn't make the adjustments required for lasting relationships. He did not accept himself or his own limitations, was proud to a fault, and his irascibility touched with arrogance made him unapproachable. He lacked the understanding of another's point of view, and felt he was right, or at least that Marx was right.

When he met the leaders of the Chinese Communist Party it was as if water had found its own level. Dr. Bethune was accepted and given the keys to the kingdom, a freedom offered only to the top echelon of the party. He could do no wrong and that, for a human being, was a big responsibility.

On the fifth day of our waiting, four trucks of the Eighth Route Army transport rolled up in front of the caves. All the children, uniforms, bedding, pots, and pans were loaded on three of the trucks, which were going northwest to Yenan. A little later our entourage boarded the remaining truck and headed for Sian. We had been on the trek for nearly a month. It was nearing the end of March. Hankow and February 1938 seemed almost as though they had never been.

CHAPTER SEVEN

Riding on top of a truck over the roads in Shensi was not the most comfortable way to see the country, especially when the melting snows had left deep ruts in the surface. The Eighth Route Army drivers had no respect for holes in the road.

In the semi-darkness we passed the great mounds of the Han and Chow graves outside the city of Sian. Soon we were confronted by high, apparently impregnable stone walls. At the gates of the city were fearful-looking guards who demanded to see our passes and passports.

Once we passed through the city gates we found the main street shops lit up and the open-fronted restaurants giving out the delicious smells one encounters only in China. The truck kept raging on, heedless of dogs, chickens, or kids, to the luxurious bath house.

Dr. Bethune went into the steam room with Lao San while I went into the door marked "Ladies." Each patron occupied a cubicle containing a king-sized tub of beautiful hot water, towels, and fragrant flower soap. After the cleaning process we all met in the front lobby.

"Well," said Dr. Bethune, "you don't look like the person who started on this junket in Hankow."

I told him that he didn't in any way resemble the dude who stepped off the *Empress* in Hong Kong.

"Jesus," he said, "it seems like a hundred years ago!"

Lao San took us via rickshaw to the Eighth Route Army headquarters where Lin Pai Chen, one of the founders of the Communist Party in China, waited to greet us. Lin and his staff were just eating. He invited us for supper, but said he had orders that we were to go to the Sian Guest House where a wonderful American meal had been ordered for us.

When we arrived at the Sian Guest House, a posh hotel for this part of the country, it took a little time to get used to the spanking white tablecloths, the cutlery and glass, the real bread and butter and cream!

Other foreigners in the dining room came over to introduce themselves: Dr. Mooser, head of the League of Nations epidemiological unit, Eric Landauer, a physicist with the unit, and a young engineer. They asked many questions relating to living conditions. Coffee and dessert lasted for several hours. Finally, the maître d' came to ask us to please leave as the hour was late–indeed it was nearly midnight.

For us the night had just started. Back at the Eighth Route Army headquarters Lin Pai Chen waited for us for more talk. He had spent many years in prison. In fact, he said he had learned his fluent English while in jail. Some of the missionaries who visited the prisons once or twice a week taught him. Lin's black eyes danced as he spoke; his spirit was youthful, despite his age and white hair. He could find many things to talk and laugh about, including himself.

Lin asked Dr. Bethune, "Where on earth did you come from? How long were you on the road? We all thought you were dead. We have even notified your people." He teased some more: "The American papers said as long as a month ago that you were lost and presumed dead." He gave us the edition of the *Chicago Tribune* dated March 12, 1938. Sure enough, the article said we were dead and ran Bethune's picture.

Lin wanted us to meet Chu Teh, who had just come in from Yenan for a conference, before the soldiers mobbed him. He was like their father and mother. The Eighth Route Army soldiers, especially the old Red Army boys, adored him. Chu Teh wore no insignia of command. Any *hsiao kuie* could hail him without reprimand. This short stocky man was the same legendary figure whose very name sent fear into the minds of the minions of the Chinese government officials as well as the Japanese.

Chu Teh was in his early fifties. His face was lined and

weather-beaten. His mouth spread in a broad grin as he greeted Dr. Bethune. They embraced. Both said, "Let me have a look at you!" each in his own language. Both laughed heartily, admiring each other as only men do when they measure up. Chu Teh, Lin, and Dr. Bethune carried on an animated conversation far into the morning. They had no need of me since Lin could speak English very well. I left them planning hospitals in Wutai Shan.

In the morning I found Dr. Bethune in a state of euphoria after his conversation with Chu and Lin. They were to have more conferences after coffee. I excused myself, saying I would like to do a little shopping and looking around.

As I walked down the streets of Sian, time seemed to stand still in the passing of history. Sian is five walled cities in one. The Empress Dowager fled here during the 1911 revolution that made China a republic. Marco Polo is said to have lived here in the days of Kubla Khan early in the twelfth century.

While I was thinking of these things, a middle-aged Swiss introduced himself as Dr. Winsler of the League of Nations, an entomologist specializing in lice. He wanted to know if I would be interested in learning about relapse fever and typhus, which were endemic, especially in war time. He strongly advised that I have typhus inoculations immediately, three shots in all, over a period of three weeks.

"I don't think we will be here that long," I told him. Dr. Bethune wanted to go north the next day if he could. Dr. Winsler insisted that I have lunch with him at the guest house.

During lunch Mr. Smythe, the Postal Commissioner, known by all as "Stamp," came over to the table.

"I guess you know you are quite a famous person now, being lost for so long," he said to me. "You even made the *Sian Daily* today–pictures and all!"

After lunch, I excused myself saying I wanted to buy a dress. I was tired of wearing a uniform and pants. I settled for a long blue sheath, Chinese style, with a lace petticoat whose gossamer scallops peeked out of the slit on each side of the skirt. I went back to the Eighth Route Army barracks wearing the outfit and feeling very lovely. Dr. Bethune met me at the door.

"Where the hell did you get that rig? It's rather out of

place," he said. I might have been without clothes judging from his displeasure.

Next morning bright and early Dr. Bethune was banging on my door. We were expected at Tung Dhi Fang, at the League of Nations epidemiological unit, for discussions on the possibility of a unit in the occupied zones and at the front where it was needed. For nearly four days we discussed sanitation, delousing, bath houses, and collecting lice, and did surveys on TB and vaccinations with these scientists. It sounded like a bizarre bit of business but the lice collecting was for serum.

Another weekend coming up. Stamp Smythe took me on a tour of Lin Tung, a few miles from Sian. Lin Tung is a spot of rare beauty, which is linked with legends and history. The eyes of the world were focused on Lin Tung in 1936 when the new China was being born. The Articles of the United Front were signed there. I saw the bullet holes in the walls–mute evidence of Chiang Kai-shek's escape in his nightshirt.

At the sulphur springs the baths were housed in a magnificent temple. The buildings were constructed with mosaic tiles of yellow and blue, filigreed windows, and a flared, gargoyled roof. When I walked around the grounds, little temples of storybook delight appeared, including man-made creeks and waterfalls spanned by toy bridges with lily ponds here and there.

Returning to Sian, Stamp's chauffeur took the long way back through the south hills. Up on a hillside, a Buddhist monk sold us a large pot of boiling water for tea. He had the self-appointed job of serving tea to wayfarers who passed, an atonement for errors and sins committed in another life. We had a picnic supper under the great cypress trees.

The next days were swallowed up by preparations to go north, first to Yenan, then across the Yellow River to the Wutai mountains where the partisans and the Eighth Route Army were beleaguered. There were purported to be 20,000 wounded in the area surrounding Wutai Shan.

We became the charges of Dr. Kiang, the chief officer of the Eighth Route Army Medical Service who had recently arrived from the Shansi front and was returning to Yenan for a

Communist Party caucus of some kind. He went to the local drug houses with Dr. Bethune to buy supplies and arrange for the transportation of all vaccines and serums that we had acquired from the League of Nations epidemiological unit.

I found Dr. Kiang a very careful man, not given to long discourses on how or why, but on getting work done. A veteran of the Long March, his family background, as well as his knowledge of organization and politics, made him most suitable for the job of medical officer. He had been involved with the Communist Party since he was a child. He trusted the party and the party trusted him in return.

I never ceased to be amazed at the unshakable belief these people had in the Communist Party and the Marxist doctrines. It was not just their faith that made them unique but their devoted selflessness to the party leadership, the Chu-Mao-Chou team. I do not possess such faith or any such capacity for absolute devotion to human beings who must have faults and foibles, to say nothing of a few sins. Dr. Bethune said it was my bourgeois upbringing that clouded my mind.

Dr. Kiang informed Dr. Bethune that there was another Canadian, Dr. Richard Brown from the Canadian mission in Kiuieteh, Honan, who would join him for a month or so in Wutai Shan.

"We will wait for him in Yenan," said Dr. Kiang.

Dr. Bethune asked many questions about Dr. Brown and his medical background. Most of all he wanted to know Dr. Brown's connection with the Communist Party. He felt that China must have strange missionaries if they were men who rendered unto God and forgot about Caesar. The missionaries would have been horrified, I am sure, at any suggestion that they should be politically involved. Politics was not part of their duties. Just how the Communist Party felt about this I do not know. However, in these times no one was in a position to refuse help, especially in the medical field.

All the articles to be transported to Yenan were loaded the night before so that only the bed rolls and personal things remained to be packed. It was not even daybreak when the trucks roared through the east gate of Sian. True to tradition,

Sian did not have a north gate, for did not all evil spirits come from the north? Once outside the gates the walls had to be circled to find the right road.

Outside the city we asked the driver to stop for a moment at the large Nestorian temple so that we might see the stone tablets written in Sanskrit that told the story of early Christians who trekked across the continent of Eurasia to escape persecution by early Roman emperors. The script is badly worn, but nevertheless the faint markings in stone tell the bitter story of when and from where the Nestorian Christians came. Like the Jews still in Kaifeng, these tablets remain as evidence of western contact with China.

Once the trucks passed the great pyramids of graves we knew that Sian was an interlude in the past, that a new life would soon await us. The countryside looked peaceful and prosperous. It was hard to imagine that a war was going on a few miles to the east beyond the Yellow River. This same sun looked down on death and desolation.

Dr. Bethune did not seem to mind travelling by truck. The three-day trek across Shansi had left him without any visible signs of fatigue, though perhaps his sojourn with General Chu Teh, commander of the Eighth Route Army, inspired him. He seemed to live within himself, his thoughts far away. He did a bit of writing on the journey, which he said he would some day rewrite as articles for Canadian newspapers and magazines. He had quite a graceful writing style and was well able to put his thoughts on paper.

The morning of the third day, the trucks were on the road very early. The drivers wanted to reach Yenan before nightfall, so they tore over the roads. Before long we were again covered with loess dust. We reached Foping, the town on the border region, and the gateway to the so-called Red regions, about ten miles from Yenan.

At Foping all passengers underwent a thorough search, certainly more trouble than crossing an international boundary. This routine, however, was quite understandable because suspicious characters now and then slipped through: not only Japanese agents but also Kuomintang disrupters.

The officer in charge went through our belongings with

minute care. At no time was he discourteous. The whole procedure for the two vehicles was over in about one and a half hours, after which we were saluted and waved on.

The road into Yenan went along the floor of the sheltered valley of the Yen River. On the sides of the barren hills the peasants were busy ploughing terraces, while the youngsters herded goats and geese. As we were nearing the end of the journey into the fabled city of the Communists, the cradle of the Chinese revolution, I must admit that I felt a little excitement mingled with some apprehension.

Long ago when the Great Wall of China was being built, the city of Yenan was the home of the overseers and their trusted slaves. The roads into the city and the walls around the city were constructed of tremendous slabs of stone. The stones were brought from far away. Not far out of Foping we could see the great tower of the south gate.

Suddenly the truck stopped again and an armed soldier examined our passes. Then he turned to Dr. Bethune saying, "Please let me look at you, for my eyes will perhaps never see such a miracle again. You have come to help us." I told Dr. Bethune to get out of the truck and say something to the lad. The small ceremony over, the guard waved us on again.

We passed through the gates of Yenan and were surprised, almost amazed, at its smallness. The dingy streets were lined with dingier stores and restaurants. The whole town had been waiting for Dr. Bethune since early morning with flags and drums. We were greeted by a kind-faced, gentle person, Dr. Mah Hai Teh, a Lebanese American from Yonkers who had come to the Red Army in Civil War days. In fact he had joined the Long March in Kansu, many miles from here.

Comrade Mah took us to supper at the newest co-operative restaurant whose specialty was coarse noodles, big fat ones. This is not a derogatory statement, but rather one of wonder, for Chinese chefs are the most adept craftsmen in the world and can camouflage noodles so that they resemble, and even taste, like something else. After eating our fill we were invited to Dr. Mah's cave for coffee. It was, he assured us, American coffee, a gift of the Japanese emperor. His convoy had fallen into the hands of the partisans, and they didn't like coffee.

This was our first coffee since Sian. To tell the truth it was a little heady at first.

While we sat around talking, Li Teh swaggered in. He was a tall, blond German national with sparse, stringy hair, watery blue eyes, and very thick glasses. He had the jaunty air of a cossack. Li Teh had been sent to China by the Russians. The Russians hadn't assisted the Chinese Red Army on their Long March, at least not with bullets or medical supplies. Instead, they sent three advisers, Li Teh among them, who could not even speak Chinese and knew little about conditions in China. It is said that the three advisers went out of their way to lose large numbers of men and equipment for the Chinese revolution. Ultimately, the infamous three were brought to trial before the tribunal of the Red Army. One of the Soviet advisers was shot, one was supposedly returned to the Soviet Union, while Li Teh was sentenced to life imprisonment. Even so, he had the freedom of the town, but was forbidden to travel beyond it without an escort.

We talked with Li Teh and Dr. Mah until well after eleven, when Buck came to tell us that we were to be settled into the guest house where everything had been made ready for us. The guest house sounds like a posh place so you can imagine my amazement when I found I didn't even have a door on my sleeping room. We had two soya-bean lamps. Rice paper was pasted over the window frames, the floor was packed earth, and the walls were freshly white-washed. A picture of Chiang Kai-shek and Madame Chiang adorned the wall. A small Kuomintang flag hung on one side of the pictures, and a large Red flag was on the opposite wall. The United Front was heavily stressed in this part of the land. They even sang about it–I guess we really were in Yenan, the new China.

I was just thinking that the next day I would take a tour around the town to see it for myself when a young man appeared in the doorway and saluted.

"Sorry to disturb you at this late hour, Comrade, but Chairman Mao requests the presence of Dr. Bethune as soon as possible." I rushed to tell Dr. Bethune that Mao Tse-tung had sent for him. The doctor was in bed, but it didn't take him a minute to dress again.

He passed my door and said, "Oh, you don't need to go."

In a very short, sarcastic manner I assured him, "Since I have not been officially expelled from this so-called medical unit, I think I am entitled to go and be represented!"

The good doctor assured me that he had not meant it in the way I understood it.

And so I went to see the Chairman of the Communist Party of China, even though I had no credentials to present. The messenger who escorted us to Chairman Mao's quarters explained that the Chairman worked during the night hours, from midnight to sometimes eight or nine in the morning when it was quiet, and that he did not usually see people unless they were important.

As we passed through the pitch-black alleys of the silent town, I was occasionally startled by sentries who shouted at the top of their lungs the old "*Shui ah!*" (who goes). The guard outside Mao's cave pushed back the heavy padded drape (there was no door) which covered the entrance. We stepped into an almost dark cavern.

Off to one side of this darkness stood a tall, lighted candle on a rough hand-hewn table. The golden light of the candle splashed over a pile of books and papers on the table, spreading up to the low ceiling of the cave, and down to the packed earthen floor. A man stood at the table with one hand resting on a book near its edge, his face turned to the door. He wore a blue cotton uniform like any other soldier in Yenan but his cap was the peaked cap with the red, five-pointed star on it. His shadow on the wall seemed to accentuate his height. The flickering shadows on the walls lent a strange quality to the scene, a murkiness broken only by the glow of the candle.

The man came towards us smiling, and in a rather high-pitched voice said, "*Hwan ying, hwan ying*–welcome, welcome." He held his hands out to Dr. Bethune, who accepted his greetings in a like manner. The Chinese leader's hands were long and sensitive, soft as a woman's. Without speaking, the two men just stared at each other for a moment, then they embraced like brothers. The chairman's face was crowned with a high forehead and a shock of very thick, unruly black hair. His sensual mouth flashed into a beaming smile as we sat down at the table where he had been working with his secretary. The secretary could speak fluent English so I was relieved of my duty. Chairman Mao spoke no language but Chinese and indeed did not seem interested in learning another tongue. After small talk about the weather, and the terrible time we must have had in Shensi, Dr. Bethune presented his credentials from the Communist Party of Canada. His card was printed on a square of white silk, signed by Mr. Tim Buck, secretary of the party, and adorned by the party seal. Chairman Mao took the credentials with great ceremony, bordering on reverence, and said, "We shall transfer you to the Communist Party of China so that you will be an inalienable part of this country now." At this point, all he asked of me was where I had learned to speak such good Chinese.

Talk as usual made its way to the Wutai mountains where the Eighth Route Army and the partisans were in need of medical care. Dr. Bethune would be a great boon to the troops over there but he wasn't sure how I would fare. It was a rough life. During the talk we drank numerous cups of tea, and ate peanuts and sunflower seeds by the handfuls: the usual fare for guests here in this barren land. Raw peanuts were cheap as well as nutritious.

After a time Mao asked me, "Don't you think that Dr. Bethune looks like V. I. Lenin?" He stood up where he could look at the doctor's profile.

"Oh yes, only Dr. Bethune has a better shaped head at the back than Lenin," I chirped brightly.

The secretary told Dr. Bethune the gist of our conversation. To say that the doctor was delighted would be to state his feelings mildly. He was flattered and pleased, even though it was a fact that at times he did look remarkably like Lenin. Eventually, the four of us got into a discussion of flat heads, and the subject took up a great deal of time without us reaching any reasonable conclusions. The night flew by on wings, and before we knew it, April second had arrived. Over the eastern hills the fingers of the dawn were pushing the darkness into eternity. Far away a rooster crowed.

Back at the guest house I dropped into bed exhausted, full of tea and peanuts. I slept until noon. By the time I wakened, Dr. Bethune had been long gone, taken by the city fathers to a banquet in his honour, in order to be greeted and welcomed to Yenan. The *hsiao kuie* said Dr. Bai had left before ten.

During the next few days Dr. Bethune had a very heavy schedule, speaking, attending banquets, giving press interviews for magazines, newspapers, and wall newspapers. He spent a lot of time with a one-armed reporter who worked for Tass, and was the only Russian national I had seen in Yenan, although the Kuomintang maintained that they were all over the place.

The afternoon saw the doctor at Kong Ta, the anti-Japanese aggression school, where he spent many hours speaking to the students and many more hours answering questions. I did not go with him, for I felt that I was living in his shadow, and that he wasn't pleased with it.

I do not know how Dr. Bethune ever kept up the pace he had set for himself. He never seemed to slacken. His credentials opened all the doors of the kingdom. He was sought out and revered as a great teacher although he considered himself a student, like all the rest of the fellows at Kong Ta–at least that's what he would say.

Each morning I took off for the border region hospital, which served a vast area because the nearest similar institution was in Sian. It also served the area to the north. It was impossible to estimate the importance of such an establishment. The Twenty-seventh unit of the Chinese Red Cross was in charge of it. My friend, Dr. Jean Chiang, seemed happy to see me, saying that she would put me to work in the operating room. This hospital was unlike any other in the world because it was all in caves. Dr. Bethune had not seen it yet and I wondered what he would think.

As far as I could see the operating rooms were as well-equipped as they could be, complete with spot lights, revolving table, and instruments in glass cupboards. But we had no running water, no sinks, no flush toilets. All scrubbing was done in great earthenware basins, which barely fitted into the kerosene sterilizer.

After three days Dr. Bethune and I were moved up the hillside from the guest house to caves of our own. I felt I should not do too much decorating for I would not live in it for long. Sleeping in a cave was a strange experience. From the bed role you hear all the chattering of the mice and the scratching of the crawlers who live in the earth. You never realize just how alive the earth is until you occupy a cave. I usually kept a light on for I did not want to be surprised by a mouse running over my feet on the way to the bread box.

During the next few days at Yenan, the border-region hospital opened a new wing to house a maternity ward, a case room, an out-patient clinic, and a sanitation unit. The case room resembled most I had worked in except for the floors and the lighting. The new caves were plastered and white-washed. There was no nursery: baskets were hung above the mother's bed so that she could nourish the baby on demand.

When Dr. Gao, the surgeon in charge of the hospital, was called away to Hankow on Red Cross business he asked Dr. Bethune to take his place at the hospital for a couple of weeks. Up to then Dr. Bethune hadn't been to the hospital but when Dr. Gao took him up to see the place he looked into one of the wards and said he damned well wouldn't work in a place like that. He declared himself on strike. He was appalled at the primitive facilities and what he considered lack of any comforts whatever. Doctors Mah and Chiang asked if he expected things to be better at Wutai Shan but he would not change his mind.

The outcome of it was that, strike or no strike, there were operations booked and Dr. Bethune performed them like the soldier he was supposed to be. He didn't like it. He wondered what was the matter with the Communists of the Soviet Union: did they not have a moral obligation as Marxists to assist their Chinese comrades? For once he didn't blame me for the conditions.

Dr. Mah explained some Chinese attitudes to him; that self-reliance meant participation by the people, and most Chinese people never had a chance to participate in anything concerning themselves before. No matter how primitive the hospital was, the fact that people survived was all that counted. When the war was over, and a Socialist China was established under the Communist Party, Dr. Mah believed that China would have the most sophisticated hospitals that could be devised. Until then, we would have to get along as best we could with what we had.

Young Mike Li was officially assigned the role of Dr. Bethune's interpreter. Mike had been one of the first Chinese boys to be sent to St. John's, the English school in Shanghai. He was a likeable fellow with an ear-to-ear grin, who, at the beginning of the war, had been given the job of organizing industrial co-ops. His English should have been sufficient for his job of interpreter but the doctor complained that he did not have the education to do this kind of work. Although Mike was willing, Bethune used too many big words and repeatedly asked Mike to translate back to English what he had said in Chinese, all of which confused the boy. Accordingly, Dr. Bethune was looking for another interpreter. But it wasn't going to be me. I had had enough!

While all this was going on a small Red Cross nurse, Miss Soong, dropped in to my cave to have a talk with me. She was in charge of the local créche. I was much impressed by the kindergarten. The compound where the children lived was very large and spotlessly clean. Their large playroom had small, child-sized tables and stools, blocks of all colours and sizes, chalk, and slate boards. There was a large sandbox in the yard, as well as swings and a slide. About fifty pre-schoolers attended. All, including the children of party functionaries, were dressed in uniforms, their faces scrubbed, their braided hair so clean that the plaits shone. They sang songs, danced, and played like most other kids. The youngsters we had brought from Shensi were also there.

One day, walking along the street with Dr. Bethune and Dr. Mah on the way to the co-op restaurant, I met the young man I had encountered in Tsinan, Shantung.

"Is it really you?" he said. "Did you know at that time that you would indeed be coming to Yenan?"

The doctors both laughed when I told them the story of this young man who, a little more than a year ago, had told me, "*Yang kuie tse!*" (go home). The lad felt very uncomfortable but I assured him that I felt no malice towards him and I hoped he felt none towards me.

The hospital was run by Dr. Nelson Foo, a man close to sixty years old, of slight build. In his gentle voice he explained to us that he had been a graduate of a missionary hospital in Chekiang province. He was proud of his fluent English. Foo had been taken prisoner along with a priest and a nun by Ho Lung on his march through Hupeh. Ho Lung needed medical aid and, being a practical man, he took it where it was available. At the time both the foreign press in Shanghai and the world press screamed about their capture. At the height of the screaming, Ho Lung's men quietly returned the nun and the priest to their mission. Dr. Foo stayed with the army voluntarily as he felt that it was the will of God that he look after the sick and wounded. He was a very devout Christian.

The nurses at the cave hospital were required to be part dietician, adding eggs, fresh produce and even milk to their patients' diets. Through experimentation, the agriculture department was able to bring more and better varieties of vegetables to the hospital. They produced giant green peppers, eggplants, and kohlrabi–vegetables that had never been grown in this part of China.

Finally the days grew longer and warmer, and we began sleeping outdoors. One morning I opened my eyes and saw the laughing face of Dr. Richard Brown who had come from the Canadian mission in Honan to go to the Wutai mountains in Shansi. Dr. Brown was a medical missionary who had spent many years in China. His family was still in Kiuieteh, Honan.

"Well, why don't you get up and greet a fellow?" he wanted to know.

When he met Dr. Brown, Bethune's first enquiry was for his supplies. He was by now somewhat worried about the things we had left in Hong Kong for the Chinese Red Cross to deliver to Yenan. It was several months since we had docked in Hong Kong and the boxes should have arrived, according to Dr. Bethune's reckoning. But he did not know that communications were more precarious in free China than they were here in the hinterland.

Dr. Brown was shown all the intriguing things around Yenan, but most of his interest lay in the public health bureau, the eye, ear, nose and throat clinic, and the latest addition, the dental clinic. He was an exceedingly polite man and would not speak anything but Chinese when a number of people were gathered. But he did explain a number of things to Dr. Bethune.

One day, the doctors and I were invited to visit the girls' brigades at the Kong Ta (anti-Japanese aggression school). This was a special privilege. It was rumoured that Chiang Ching, who later became the chairman's wife, was to be a student there.

As we approached the caves, a girl sentry presented arms. We were met and escorted by two teachers who directed the whole operation. Hundreds of young women from every province in China were enrolled here. Most were healthy and rosy, dressed in soldiers' uniforms, clamouring to ask questions about our country. We saw all the dormitories, the kitchens, and classrooms that also served as dining rooms. Each cave housed ten students and even though it was a little bit crowded at times, they did not seem to mind. The walls were covered with very fine caricatures of the different leaders drawn by the girls themselves.

The students informed us that they mapped out their own curriculum with the help of the teachers. I asked why most women in China today wore uniforms. One sweet youngster answered that it was "due to the lack of dye and cloth." She went on to say that because communications were unreliable most people in occupied China and some parts of so-called free China found it more convenient to wear uniforms. They were readily available and at the moment fashionable. Personally, I thought women preferred them because they were cheap and easy to care for. Even old housewives and small children wore them.

There was another burning question that also concerned me. I took one of the teachers aside and asked, "How do you manage as far as periods are concerned?"

She looked at me a little shocked and said, "Well, the way we have always managed." This wasn't enough for me. So she went into greater detail, telling me that they procured very porous wheat husk paper because it was more absorbent, and not much different from the cellulose that made up our napkins.

The students were very interested in the student movements in the United States and wondered if they were mostly YMCA and YWCA or church-sponsored groups. It was difficult to explain that student movements in other countries, especially in the United States, had no real depth and no real connection with economic forces reshaping society.

In old China, education was only for the privileged classes. If a peasant or worker wished to send his child to school it meant some privation for the whole family. Whatever the costs, parents were glad to pay. Old China had a reverence for learning, but in the new China, through the medium of the Communist Party, opportunities to acquire a socialist education would be on a gratis basis.

After the school visit I went exploring on my own and met Dr. Yetmar, a bacteriologist working with the League of Nations Sanitation Corps in Yenan, who was doing research on bubonic plague. His interests were also in botany and entomology. He was collecting the flora of north Shensi. At his shanty in Yenan, he showed me his files of beautifully pressed specimens of flowers, bugs, and butterflies, all native to north Shensi. The villagers had come to think Dr. Yetmar a bit strange, for only feeble-minded men bothered about such insignificant things. They could not perceive that some time in the future, people might want to know what it was like in Shensi in 1938.

With the Sanitation Corps, Dr. Yetmar was a hard taskmaster and would march them all around the town to see that all the latrines were properly limed and cleaned.

Doctors Brown and Bethune received an invitation to see Chairman Mao. Dr. Brown, I believe, was deeply impressed for he did not expect to find the chairman so mild and gentle. He was remembering the accounts in the capitalist paper. I told him he should feel honoured for the chairman only saw people he considered important.

The propaganda department of the party sent us tickets to

the movies. What do you know? Real talking pictures made their debut here! The town was bustling with excitement and anticipation, especially since the movies were to be in the open air in the Yamen or courthouse grounds. The donkey engine from the X-ray department was set up on the veranda of one of the houses while the screen was placed in an appropriate spot under the eaves of a blank wall of another house across the courtyard. Benches were placed; but long before dark there wasn't standing room for even a flea. The owners of roofs on the adjoining houses sold tickets to anyone wishing to buy. Farmers came from far and near to see this new wonder of science–an old Soviet western.

After the show, Chairman Mao gave a small speech and introduced the two new doctors and the nurse who had come to help the wounded. The crowd thumped and clapped and then one of the little soldiers wanted to hear the doctors sing a Canadian song. Dr. Bethune sang "Joe Hill." They were then told by Dr. Brown who Joe Hill was. The audience was very responsive and clapped in unison.

On my return to my cave, Doctors Mah, Brown, and Bethune were waiting for me. They wanted me to go back to Sian to buy as many supplies of anaesthesia, narcotics, pills, and bandages as I could lay my hands on. I did not think much of the idea but they insisted I should go because I was the youngest and Dr. Brown was not yet rested from his trip. We needed the drugs but the question was could I make it before the big rains.

The second day out of Yenan the rains started. It is difficult to imagine the depth of Shensi mud. Just before we reached the gates of Sian, the drivers helped pull two trucks out of the mud. Lo and behold, there on the trucks were our boxes from Hong Kong.

At the Sian guest house I met Captain Evens Pfordyce Carlson, naval attaché to the American embassy. I mistook him for a missionary in his shorts and pith helmet, and when he said, "I think you must be Jean Ewen," I must have looked as though I were going to run. But the Captain brought letters and mail for me, the first I had had since I had returned to China. I found him a good companion and a good sport. He was going to Suiyuan to see Mah Chon Shan and of necessity would travel to Yenan with me and then north to the Yellow River.

When I returned to Yenan, I found that the good doctors had stripped my cave of everything, including my foodstuffs. Before I could find out what had happened, Carlson suggested that we take part in the May Day celebrations, for who knew when we would see another May Day in China.

Long before dawn, the tramp of marching men on the highways resounded through the hills. The echo of their songs rang wave on wave in the morning air, the sound bouncing off the highest hills to re-echo in the valleys. Every citizen, to the last child, turned out in their best clothes and their best holiday spirit. The town was garbed in festive decorations: flags, bunting, and slogans in red and gold. Games, dances, and plays were all part of the celebrations.

Chairman Mao spoke to the crowd for a full three hours. The chief of staff presented prizes to the different brigades who won contests in the field day. Captain Carlson held forth with a speech for another hour. Then both of us were wined and dined royally by students and soldiers alike. At the end of the day, we watched a Soviet western, *If War Should Come Tomorrow*. Peddlers and hawkers did a roaring business in candies, cigarettes, and biscuits.

Dr. Mah invited Carlson and me to his cave for coffee after the show, for he felt he had to explain why all my goods were gone. He didn't make a good job of it, and I was at my most aggravating, splitting hairs, looking stony, or saying nothing.

Mah finished off by informing me that I would be continuing on with Captain Carlson.

CHAPTER EIGHT

Two days later, Captain Carlson and I met down at the quartermaster's shack for the journey northward with a company of twenty-five students returning to occupied Shansi for work in the political education of peasants. The drivers carried mail, which was some weeks late on account of heavy rain. By afternoon we reached a sleepy little town called Yen Ping.

A few miles out of the town we came upon the skeletons of oil derricks long since silent. The shafts had been drilled, oil brought up, and now the pumps were idle. The equipment belonged to Socony Standard Oil Company of New York. There were several shacks on the premises for engineers and technicians that had wooden floors and the remnants of glass windows. The driver explained that since the Red Army moved in nothing had been done to pump the crude from the ground. The Socony boys left papers and even time-sheets in their wake.

Back on the road, progress was slow because of the winding hairpin turns and the ankle-deep loess dust, which came up from the rear wheels like a fountain, saturating everything. On the climb up one hill, the old truck conked out, and would not go despite all our coaxing, cursing, and clucking. The gas pump was out of commission so we sat in the sun again for a couple of hours while the mechanic attempted to repair it. Finally, in desperation, the mechanic removed the bonnet, perched himself on the front fender, and with the aid of a can of gas and a small hose, spoon-fed the old motor.

This necessitated travelling at a snail's pace and taking the bumps very easily lest we dislodge the mechanic. We went some ten miles at this impossible pace when the mechanic spotted a cluster of caves and decided to stop there to work on the old truck. We were not even halfway to Ching Chan.

The hamlet, a quaint forgotten place that boasted four families, was delighted at the prospect of making a few dollars on such a handsome company. The mistress of the house where we stayed could not believe her eyes. Only once, when she was a small child, had she seen a foreigner but now she had two staying with her. Soon all the women in the settlement gathered to have a look at the strange phenomenon: me. The women were pathetically illiterate and spoke an awful colloquial dialect so they were not easy to understand.

Our hostess had come from a neighbouring village as a bride at twelve years of age. She had had eight pregnancies but only one baby survived–a boy of seven who was her pride and joy. She had never left her home, not even to go to Yenan. The soldiers of the Eighth Route Army considered her quite intelligent. At least she knew there was a war. Most villagers in the hinterland were not aware of this. Our hostess's son, a ragged, scabby-headed urchin, hung around displaying his knowledge. He knew all about the war and what should be done about it. He could read a newspaper and could write 200 characters and went to school for six months of the year. He went into the family cave and emerged a few minutes later with a volume wrapped in a piece of blue cloth. He was pleased to tell us that this book told all about the lands from which we came. He called it *Hai Wai Hsien Hwa*, Grimm's Fairy Tales!

At noon the next day we stopped at a village for lunch. The inn did not look very inviting but since there was not another village till Ching Chan we took advantage of it, if just for a pot of tea. The cook, by the look of him, hadn't come in contact with soap and water for some time. Certainly his clothes, especially his apron, had never been washed. He carried a grimy, greasy cloth at his side, which he waved around, wiping off tables, cups, dishes, and frying pans impartially. After these operations he put the cloth into a dirty wash basin of greasy water, wrung it out, and mopped his face and shaven head.

Big bluebottle flies seemed to be on convention here, for they buzzed all over the place, from the dog's back to the baby's face to the food. I had qualms about the kind of infection the baby might be exposed to with all this contamination. The Sanitary Corps was certainly needed in a place like this.

After lunch we roared off again and soon arrived in Ching Chan. My old friend Buck appeared to meet us. Captain Carlson and I parted here, each to go our separate ways, promising that we would meet in Shanghai at Christmas time. Buck said arrangements had been made for me to stay at the Medical Bureau, but when I got there I found no one at home. After a long wait, Dr. Liu, the doctor-cum-soldier in charge of the post came in, very apologetic that he had been so long.

Ching Chan was a supply station with all the hospital supplies and equipment necessary for the front's clearing stations and field hospitals. Dr. Wong Bin, a Szechwanese, came over to introduce himself and to ask a favour, not a big one, you understand. Would I help catalogue the entire stock of the caves stuffed with medical and surgical supplies, dressings, and instruments, and list them all in block lettering? The small favour took the better part of two weeks for both the doctor and I, working from breakfast to suppertime every day.

When I gave him the lists he bowed and said, "Now you must teach me English and I will teach you Chinese." He was smiling placidly as though he were asking for a drink of water. I protested that I already had a good working knowledge of his language and in a few weeks expected to leave Ching Chan, so it would not be possible for him to acquire much English. Besides we had no books. But he was insistent and so we had English lessons.

In due time I was introduced to the rear hospital of the 120th Division. The nurses were all boys, and I do mean boys, for the youngest was just fourteen years of age, the eldest sixteen. But they were willing and eager. Dr. Wong cheerfully told me that they had their full course in theory but he would appreciate it if I would give them the practical side of nursing. Their education generally was very elementary and their knowledge of Chinese characters was on a level with my own. I did my very best to make them good dressers for the units going into action.

Nearly a month went by, during which time these youngsters initiated a campaign on flies, started an inoculation station for cholera and measles, and even formed a sanitation corps.

During my stay at Ching Chan I was allowed to witness the trial of a deserter. Where the lad was deserting to is something I could not answer, for this area of Shensi was thinly populated; and towns were not very big, making it impossible to hide in them. At the appointed time, four soldiers took the prisoner out of the cave that served as a jail. In lieu of handcuffs, both his arms were tied with a piece of clothesline rope. Another piece of clothesline was tied around his neck and he was led in this humiliating way to meet his Waterloo. The Chinese have such humiliating methods of treating criminals that no one wants to ever get caught in that predicament.

All members of the military and medical bureaus were present with Dr. Liu in the chair, the presiding judge so to speak. Very pompously he hammered the table with a gavel, which brought the business to order. He explained that Comrade Chow Tse Tseng, employed as a water carrier for the kitchens, did two nights ago desert his post. He would now have a chance to defend himself, for this was very serious business–it could have left the base without water, maybe even without food. Twisting the prisoner's arm a little more he pointed out that there were patients in the hospital who might have been distressed–all ten of them. The villagers and personnel of Ching Chan were the judges and jury and discussed at length the water carrier's crime. A unanimous vote found him guilty as charged. He was sentenced to carry water for three months without leave or pay. He was also warned that next time he would be handed over to the authorities at Yenan.

After the proceedings, Dr. Liu and I decided to take the long way back. We came upon a cluster of houses that I wanted to see. A few children played in the yards and some women were sunning themselves while sewing. They had the tiniest feet I had ever seen, scarcely three inches from heel to the tip of the shoe. Their hair style must have been very old-fashioned for I had not seen one like it before. Great silver stick pins held an intricately wound roll in place at the nape of the neck. Their clothes also came from the last century, while their houses were filled with antiques that would have delighted the tender heart of any dealer.

Going by one of the gates of a compound we noticed burning joss sticks around the outside of the door. The gates were open so we walked in. Such brazen curiosity in the backwoods of China was accepted etiquette. From the inner darkness of the room a weird chanting kept getting louder and louder. Meanwhile the lady of the house came to see what we wanted.

"What's all the fuss about?" I asked her.

"My son is ill. The medicine man has come to bring back his spirits," she answered quite simply.

"Can we help?" Dr. Liu asked. Edging closer to the door of the sickroom we were transported back a few centuries in superstition. There was a medicine man, exorcist if you wish, with his face painted in streaks of white, yellow, red, and blue. He wore a yellow and red paper crown on his head with golden characters on it. Fascinated, I watched his weird and wonderful gyrations. Surely my eyes were deceiving me–a bowl on the table began whirling around and slowly rising in the air. So, too, was the medicine man. Many turnabouts later he stopped, picked up a meat cleaver, and waved it through the air at a terrific rate, beating his scrawny chest with the flat side. This performance he repeated many times. Then he got down on his knees to do a full kotow three times. Rising to his feet, he seized the cleaver and mumbled, then flung it out the door across the yard. Lighting more joss sticks he stuck them into the wall above the head of the sick man.

The ceremony was now over. If the patient's soul did not

return before sunrise he would surely die. The medicine man left a charm, which he would want back when the patient recovered; otherwise it stayed with him. I asked to see what was in the charm. The medicine man obliged cheerfully. There were feathers from a newly hatched chick, a couple of bones, teeth from a dog, a frog's leg, and lots of shredded paper. The affair cost the family two dozen eggs and three pounds of meat, usually one good-sized chicken. I learned later that these deals are strictly barter.

"How did you make the bowl spin and yourself also?" I asked. He said he didn't know, but he had realized he had these powers since he was about seven years old. His grandfather also had this ability, and he could tell the colour of paper while blindfolded. He was seldom wrong. But the medicine man could not do the thing he wanted to do: read and write.

As we walked back to the town I asked Dr. Liu, "Why doesn't he call a proper doctor?"

"This is a matter of his own choice," insisted Dr. Liu.

"Well, Comrade, I would think the Army would do something about this kind of superstition," I ventured.

Dr. Liu was very patient with me, saying that he did not expect me to understand the policy of the Red Army–which was not to interfere with the life and customs of the peasants. But no doubt in the future they would explore the whys and the wherefores of how a man totally illiterate could cause an object to become airborne.

During the evening wounded soldiers from the Nineteenth Provincial Army passed through on their way back to their rear hospital. They had been on the road nearly three weeks. Their story was of pain, hunger, and exposure; and their wounds were septic and often gangrenous. The lucky ones had adequate covering but most of them wore uniforms crusted with dirt and blood, and many were lousy. The wounded, emaciated beyond imagination, were draped on boards just wide and long enough to accommodate a body. The boards were suspended on ropes from a pole which could be carried by two other men. The Nineteenth Army hospital was situated on the other side of Ching Chan. Dr. Wong Bin went personally to offer assistance and medicine.

Shortly after midnight I was called to help a patient in labour in a small settlement a mile away. The man who came said his baby refused to be born. With much difficulty, I used forceps to deliver a bouncing boy of nearly eight pounds, which is huge for a Chinese bairn. The mother, however, was not in such good condition, mainly because of overwork and undernourishment.

When I did not show up for hospital rounds in the morning, Dr. Wong came looking for me. When I told him I had delivered a child in the night, he demanded to know why I had not called him. I knew he was in charge and responsible for all movements of the staff and I knew he was angry because he had never had a delivery and probably would not know what to do with a pair of forceps.

Later that day, I had my first glimpse of tetanus infection, commonly called lockjaw, in an adult. The patient had broken his leg and had a compound fracture with the bones sticking through the broken skin. It was a dirty-looking mess, nearly two days old. When I asked Dr. Wong about anti-tetanus serum he only laughed at me in his ignorance. He proceeded to set the fracture. Towards the evening the man's temperature shot up to 103°. His neck began to stiffen, and soon he could not talk for his jaws would not open. A little more than twelve hours later he was dead. His young wife was beside herself with grief. It happened too suddenly for her to comprehend.

Spring had melted into the middle of June and I was no closer to Shansi. This was not the way I wanted it. I visited Dr. Liu to ask about a pass to Ho Lung's headquarters. He said it was my lucky day for one of Dr. Mah's trucks would be passing through the next morning for Yulin, so I could go as far as Shui Teh with it. He felt that four or five of the nurses were experienced enough to go out as dressers with the front units of the partisans.

The trucks came at six in the morning, stopped just long enough to have tea, and then we were away. The road to Shui Teh was almost a continuous climb. The mountains became wilder and without habitation. After what seemed an endless ride we were confronted with city gates although the city itself was very small. I was surprised to find my old friend, the adjutant from Tungkuan, at the Eighth Route Army headquarters in Shui Teh. He pumped my hand vigorously saying, "*Aye Ya, Tung Chih*, so you have come back to cause me some more trouble–once to Shansi isn't enough?"

We talked of Dr. Bethune, of our visit to Tungkuan–the old man and his leg, and of how long the trip back took us. Suddenly he said, "Oh yes, I have some letters for you. They have been here for quite a long time." One of the letters had a very official Chinese government letterhead and was signed by one of Madame Chiang's advisers. It stated that it was illegal for me to work except under the direction of Madame Chiang herself, and I would be arrested if I didn't comply with the edict. I had to answer it while I was still mad enough to put down what I felt. I told the adviser if Madame wanted me so badly she could come and get me. The other letter was from Dr. Bethune. In it he told me that he felt the life was too rough and I was too young to go on a mission such as this. He also wrote that I did not understand the gravity or seriousness of the cause that I served. The bloody missionary! He enclosed copies of letters written to Canada to ask for money so I could get home, plus a letter to Mao Tse-tung asking him to see that I got home. Who the hell did he think he was anyway? I tore both letters into small pieces.

A young Szechwanese girl cadre, Ling, invited me to her quarters where I spent a very pleasant evening and was her guest for the next couple of days.

After two days of rest we were on the road again. In the early morning the green world was beautiful, every branch laden with dew that sparkled in the morning sunlight like jewels. Now it was time to go down the mountain to cross the Yellow River. Sometimes the path was so steep that you could hardly stand up straight. At the river's edge we got on a barge that was already loaded with animals, soldiers, and tons of cargo. When all was settled, the barge left for the Shansi side. The crossing took the better part of two hours.

Long after lunch we reached the Army compounds, which were buzzing with life. An old Red Army man was in command of the post. He assured us he had ordered a good supper for us so now we must rest and clean up. I was escorted to the dwelling of a family who kept a number of goats, two of them milk goats. Their children ate goat cheese, drank goat's milk, and ate carrots like candy. The whole dozen of them looked rosy and healthy. This was a Catholic household, and when all chores were done the family assembled in the courtyard, where the old grandfather led in counting the beads and saying the litany of the angels. It was a long time since I had heard the familiar "Hail Mary" in Chinese and the *Wie Wo Dung Chi* response to the litany. It brought back memories of long ago. There was only one thing wrong with the place. It was crawling with bedbugs, which left me with large bumps all over. I felt I needed an extra day to rest and do something about my bites.

The comings and goings at this post were fantastic; wounded coming in with another transport, or mule skinners waiting to be paid. Most of them squatted around on their haunches drinking tea and smoking, or telling tales of their trips into the occupied zone.

The wounded were from the field hospital at Lanhsien. Their wounds were healed but since their convalescence was not completed they were on leave. Some were a little uncomfortable since they had not had leave since the war started.

When we left, a company of singing soldiers preceded the convoy in case we should come upon the enemy. They kept about a mile ahead of the first pack animals. The 120 pack animals, laden mostly with ammunition, were an impressive sight.

Approaching a hill, three soldiers and a mule skinner suddenly dashed for the other side of the road and scrambled up the hill on all fours. All were doing a great deal of shouting, yelling, and scuffling, in the midst of which a shot rang out. About ten minutes later the soldiers came back, with a wild boar, feet in the air, suspended from a stout tree branch. They were laughing and joking. Meat for supper–what else?

Shansi is indeed a very beautiful province especially in the early morning. On the hillsides high above the road were a profusion of wild lilacs, magnolias, and wild orchids in green and brown. There was little human habitation here–only birds and animals who chattered noisily. As we travelled along, the hills got a little higher, or maybe we were a little more tired.

As we proceeded we could hear the droning hum of bombers. The adjutant shouted, "*Shan kai*" (separate, take cover). The animals were led into the castor plants and hemp without much confusion. Nine bombers passed over at scarcely 2000 feet. Their silver wings glistened in the noonday sun.

Soon we were on our way again, to cross a marshland. Off to the north a thunderstorm was on its way. Quickly, animals and cargo were covered with oilskins carried on the first three animals. Rain came down in sheets.

We were beginning to dry out just as we reached the stopping-off place at sunset. Lin was just another village with the usual swarms of flies and dogs. As we were eating our noodles who should come through the door but the chief medical officer, Dr. Kiang. He was horrified that I was so sunburned–if I laughed I felt my face would crack. He had gotten Doctors Bethune and Brown to Wutai in good time. While they were crossing the Japanese lines in total darkness, Dr. Bethune's typewriter had been lost.

"Did he scream?" I enquired, laughing.

"Did he ever," answered Dr. Kiang, "but it all turned out fine because when they got to headquarters the typewriter was sitting on the table."

CHAPTER NINE

June was nearly over when our transport arrived at Lanhsien city, Ho Lung's headquarters. The adjutant soon had us standing outside the commander's door waiting for an interview. We could hear our adjutant announce himself, then tell Ho Lung that he had brought ammunition, canned beef, medical supplies, soldiers, summer clothing, five dressers, and a foreign woman.

"What!" exclaimed a heavy masculine voice.

"A foreign woman," calmly announced the adjutant. The little devil then ushered us into the sanctum sanctorum of the two-headed dragon, Ho Lung, commander of the 120th Division of the Eighth Route Army.

Giving me the once over he asked: "You know who I am, eh?"

"You are the man who captured two missionaries in Hupeh and brainwashed them," I replied, having been told that this subject usually broke the ice with Ho Lung. I asked him if it were true that he let the missionaries preach to the Red Army men.

"Sure," he replied, "they were good people."

Ho Lung, the double-headed dragon, the man of many names, mostly derogatory, stood squarely before me, not very tall, broad of shoulder, and all rebel. His face was square, he had heavy eyebrows, flashing black eyes, a wide sensuous mouth and on the upper lip, a sparse moustache of which he was proud. In his mouth he held a black cigarillo, which was seldom lit, but which travelled from one side of the mouth to the other during an interesting conversation. A very young fifty, he walked with grace, and the litheness of a cat. During the National Revolution his troops were incorporated into the Chinese armies.

I asked him if it were true that he had captured a motor launch from the Kuomintang armies, which was now called Ho Lung's Navy. The launch was used to scoot over the lakes and direct guerrilla war against the Kuomintang.

For years, Ho Lung had tried to join the Communist Party of China, and after ten tries he was finally accepted. He could read and was schooling himself in the classical written language. Outwardly he was hard as a rock but once this shell was broken, he was said to be a real softie.

Hsiao Ke, the Vice-Commander and political commissar, entered saying that he had just heard there was a foreign woman with Ho Lung, of all things! Hsiao Ke was a wiry, neurotic sort of fellow, who talked very quickly, jumped around a lot, and waved his hands as he talked. I believe if his hands were amputated he would not have been able to speak. Younger than Ho Lung, in his late thirties or early forties, Hsiao Ke was handsome except for his acne. He was trying to coax a few whiskers out of his chin but they didn't want to grow.

The officers debated where I should stay because they didn't want me around the barracks. The commander sent for Thou Dung, a young woman of my own age–a teacher by day and a theatrical director in her spare time. She entered the room with a puzzled look on her face while Ho Lung explained the situation to her saying, "This *Yang kuie tse* has come to look after our wounded. Take her, and see that she gets everything she needs." From this time on, I became known without malice as the *Yang kuie tse*; villagers and soldiers alike called me this.

The first night in Lanhsien, I had been in bed only a short while when an annoying, persistent knock on my door aroused the household. Imagine my surprise when I was confronted by a ragged peasant in a Japanese greatcoat. Winter issue in the middle of summer. His arms were loaded with goodies like American coffee, cigarettes, biscuits, and runny chocolates. He said his partisan unit had captured a Japanese transport of some twenty trucks laden with supplies and comforts. He saluted me and was gone. Next day in the compound of the headquarters were truck tires, wheels, batteries, or any truck part you could want. The parts that could be used were kept. The unusable metal was chopped up and sent back to the Japanese Army in cannon shells, which could include everything from horseshoe nails to truck fenders.

After loafing for two wonderful days I finally caught up with some work. The medical centre was a mile and a half away from where I lived. There was no hospital so patients were quartered with the peasants or townspeople. The heavily wounded were housed within a radius of a mile and were brought to the station for surgery. They would stay in the compound until they could be moved. The station had three doctors, five dressers who took the place of nurses, and a pharmacist, all under Army Medical Service. There were also twenty students taking dressers' courses, first and second class. A first-class dresser was a person trained to go out with the troops, set bones, give sedation and hypos, and take bullets out of wounds. A second-class dresser worked around the hospital assisting the doctors and sterilizing instruments.

Dr. Jong was in charge. He complained that his training was far from adequate but he got lots of practical experience! He wanted to take a course in emergency surgery so he could go to the front. I wondered what he meant. This *was* the front. Any closer and we would be where the soldiers were fighting.

At the present moment, Dr. Jong had a bad case of girl trouble. His girlfriend would not say yes to his tender pleas. She was one of the army girls but she wanted all the flim-flammery ordinary brides have. Dr. Jong insisted she shouldn't be interested in such things for the new China did not have time for it.

Dr. Li needled him about applying partisan tactics. Dr. Li, formerly a Red Army prisoner and a native of Hunan, joined the Medical Corps of the old Red Army because he had had considerable training in a mission hospital near his home. He said he liked the Army, especially its discipline, where men and soldiers mixed together without fear. Since the United Front, he had brought his wife and six-year-old son to Yenan. His wife taught in the elementary school, and his son, a young pioneer, looked forward to being a chemical engineer. An amazing number of people in the Eighth Route Army Medical Corps had at one time or another been connected with the foreign missions. They had been in their schools, or trained in mission hospitals, or been contacted in jails.

Wu, the pharmacist, was a very young man about nineteen or twenty and his knowledge of *materia medica* left a lot to be desired. He could barely read or understand the Latin names on the drug bottles.

Outside of the bare necessities and essentials, there was practically no equipment. Sulpha drugs were unheard of; penicillin had not yet been discovered, but many native medications were used. The centre had a large stock of ether and novocaine powder, so I instructed the pharmacist in how to make a proper solution, how to distil water, and in how to follow Dr. Bethune's method of cutting raw opium for hypodermic injection.

The operating rooms had regulation Red Cross disaster kits of instruments. More than half of these had never been used. In my search of the cupboards I found a beautiful set of obstetrical instruments, which we used later. New sterilizers were badly needed. The old kitchen table-cum-operating table should have been replaced for the legs weren't of the same length. The doctors and I wrote a manual of procedures for changing dressings, taking out bullets, setting simple fractures, and delivering babies. These would prove useful to the dressers still in training. Organizing the manual was done after the regular day's work.

The Medical Corps had a war going on against flies and dirt. They set up cholera inoculating stations as it was dysentery time. Their largest project was a bath house and delousing station. Dr. Jong and I insisted that the bath houses could not be delayed because the patients had to be housed with the peasants. We felt that peasants' homes should be fumigated and their bedding inspected and that the Army must give the peasants the same consideration as the patients. The bath house was to be open to the public one day a week.

The only hospitalization available in this area was offered by the Eighth Route Army. Attached to the medical centre was an out-patient dispensary where people came at any time of the day. Consequently we worked long hours. The medical personnel divided the area into four sections with each of the three doctors assigned to one section. I was assigned the fourth section.

There were some patients with messy wounds in my section. Their dressings took a long time and sometimes the dresser who went with me would have to go back for more supplies. I did not complain, although the dresser did. One patient was a Japanese prisoner, Nichi, we called him for convenience. He could not be quartered with the peasants but had been confined at the centre with a stinking belly wound. His temperature was very high with all the accompanying symptoms of major infection. Dr. Jong decided he would have to operate on him and when he made the incisions he found a Japanese coin all done up in a muscle sheath in the abdominal wall, gift-wrapped in a rare smelling abscess. After a couple of weeks we turned Nichi loose for the Army to re-educate. We communicated with him by means of Chinese characters and sign language, but soon the whole staff was picking up Japanese phrases. Nichi eventually got around to helping with dressings and doing the dirty work around the medical centre.

One thing I was curious about was whether the peasants ever considered the wounded who were billeted in their homes a nuisance or burden. I asked one lady if our patients were much trouble in her home. She said that while they were bed patients it was a bit of "*mah fan*" (inconvenience) but once they were on their feet, they helped out by looking after the small children, washing dishes, even helping with the washing and weaving. Then I asked her if they didn't sometimes quarrel? She looked at me strangely and said, "Sure, but who in the world doesn't quarrel at one time or another."

One hellishly hot night, shortly after midnight, Dr. Jong

and I delivered a pair of twins to a young peasant woman. I said it was the first pair of twins I had ever delivered in all my years in China. "Better late than never," was his reply, as he told me he had never delivered a child before. He thanked me for teaching him what to do. Next time he wouldn't fumble. He tied the cords with a knowing air, instilled silver nitrate in the small eyes, and wrapped the pair in part of a blanket. We left the mother comfortable with her double happiness of two sons.

For meals the staff congregated at the headquarters where everyone was served at two long tables. After meals we all gathered at the recreation field to play tennis or volleyball, popular sports there, especially for the girls. The courts were in fine condition. Horse racing was also popular. The animals were brought to the field and saddled up.

Ho Lung once offered me his stallion. I think he wanted to see me dumped, but much to his surprise I made it into the saddle right side up. The animal went round and round the clearing, snorting, pawing and kicking. When he decided that maybe I wasn't going to get off, he settled into a nice canter, but before long, he stopped dead and would not move. Ho Lung said I was the first woman to ever ride him and I knew the horse didn't like it.

On the field were two veterans of the Long March, an old plug and a mule.

"Two things the Red Army did not lose on the Long March were mules and women," Ho Lung explained teasingly. "Not one woman or mule listed as a casualty." The statement was not only chauvinistic, it wasn't exactly true.

Then the commander said he was about to show me his special feat–the like of which I would probably never see again. One of the *hsiao kuie* blew the air warning signal. The horses started to prance around, their riders dismounted, drawing the reins up over the horses' heads securely. Meanwhile, the animals dropped to one knee, then the other knee, then each lowered its hindquarters to the ground and rolled over on one side lying flat on the ground. Until the all clear sounded they stayed put. Then as soon as the trumpet blasted the one long note they were up on their feet in a flash.

On July 7, 1938, the first anniversary of the fall of Marco Polo Bridge was commemorated with a great mass meeting. Before eight in the morning, the crowd of armed soldiers in shorts, armed civilians in their cotton clothes, and some of the old timers still wearing their long braids, was assembled out in the clearing beyond the city walls. Colourful indeed were the Red spearmen, each carrying long ugly-looking weapons with a red ribbon tied under the blade. The women's brigades also had spears. It was all very impressive when one stopped to consider that Japanese troops were within a day's march of the town. Then came the speeches. I had come to the conclusion that the Eighth Route Army had the champion speechmakers in the whole universe. If someone could not make a speech last an hour then he had no merit. Even the oldsters had a crack at it. They did not mind telling young folks just what was wrong with them and how it could be remedied.

In these so-called occupied areas there was no such thing as a refugee. The population became part of the Army, part of a civilian force that did not wander into the unknown part of free China. The industries were on a small scale so that they could be dismantled and moved at the drop of a Japanese hat. When the Japanese Army decided to move in some direction, the people of that area moved all their belongings–livestock, children, grain, chickens, along with the co-operative industries which they worked at during the time they were dislocated–to the hills. If the Japanese were driven back, the peasants moved home again with their possessions. I was astonished to see so many co-ops flourish in this so-called occupied territory.

The official stamp of the co-ops was a triangle with the characters Gung Ho in the centre. A little soldier explained to me that the three sides of the triangle stood for the three principles of Sun Yat-sen: nationalism, democracy, and the people's livelihood. These people were not building for today or the next year but for the whole future of China. A thousand years from now the people of Shansi would know Chairman Mao.

Each co-operative had its own reading room, dining room,

and kitchens. One of the women I chatted with stated that work had opened up a whole new world for her, the world of books and papers. Six months before, she couldn't write her own name or read a newspaper. The co-op had a teacher on hand for several hours a day so that all who wished to study could do so. Another advance for these women was that husbands weren't allowed to collect their wives' pay cheques. For the first time in their lives, wives had money of their own to spend as they pleased.

Here at the 120th in Lanhsien, the dramatic groups gave a good account of themselves in some nearly professional performances. Sometimes sound and action did not synchronize, so that a man fell dead before the gun report sounded, but it made for a good laugh. The youngsters put on a sketch, a takeoff on the medical centre, which had us work on a patient with hammers, butcher knives, and screw drivers. The anticlimax came when the patient got too enthusiastic, knocked over a candle backstage, and somebody shouted "Fire!" Then everyone moved. The young actor who played the role of me was quite good. No mistaking my being white, bulging in all the right places. Only the backside slipped occasionally down the leg of his pants. Many a smile crossed his face as he adjusted the posterior.

One afternoon in August, the commander came to the medical centre, something he rarely did. He said there had been a great deal of fighting to the northeast. Partisans were wounded and he wanted a few of us to go. We all jumped at the chance.

We were to start after the heat of the day was over and no one was to go beyond the marked territory. Around five, kits conveniently packed, Doctors Jong, Li, a dresser, and I mounted horses and headed away. Orders were followed. We stayed a long way behind the vanguard of soldiers ahead. Along the way, peasants asked for medicines for scabies and trachoma, or to have wounds treated. Measles were on the rampage among the children. Practically every house was inflicted and there were many complications. Some of the youngsters were blind or nearly blind, some had edema of the legs and feet and heart complications. Everywhere malnutrition was the biggest problem. There was not enough to eat, and not enough money to buy food which wasn't available anyway. The distress of the civilians in this bloody war was extreme, although in some places it had always been so. We tried to talk "isolation" to the women as a solution to the epidemic but they did not understand.

The wounded civilians were happy to see us. There were no doctors or missionaries to help them. The appalling poverty in this wealthy, wealthy land was beyond belief. It beggars words to describe it. I wondered what it would be like in fifty years. Conditions couldn't possibly be worse.

Next morning we started on our way early to a town called Si Mah Pu. The countryside was not unlike Lin Fen farther south. All at once we were aware of a terrible odour, a stink that got worse with every step. Four soldiers came galloping up and insisted that we must go no farther, adding that there was no one around, nothing we could do anyway. Doctors Li and Jong were ready to turn back, but I wanted to see the gift of the Imperial Army.

A buzzing silence hung over the town. Windows of empty houses gaped like holes in a skull. We decided the best place to start was the church compound. Inside the big gate, slumped against the wall, the dead doorkeeper stood guard. Alongside him a girl, probably a catechist, was shot through the head. Their clothes were crusted, and their faces and hands were turning black. The odour was intense. Inside the compound, behind the church, were several bodies of old people in grotesque positions. Nearby, two small corpses were thrown in a pig trough. Everything in the small church had been broken-windows, chairs, books, dishes, and vestments. The vigil light was filled with human excrement. Then the light had been hung around the neck of a statue of Saint Theresa. The good earth was indeed sick. Horse dung littered the floors. The resident missionary was not around.

The doctors instructed the soldiers to move out. We decided not to go any farther as the newly wounded were now reaching us. No one felt in the mood for eating but the peasants who lived outside the village gave us wine and *hsiao bings*, saying food would do us good. These peasants seemed to think that the missionary had been taken by the Japanese soldiers. The priest was from *Ho Lan Kuo* (Holland). The peasants were sure that no harm could come to the missionary because he was a foreigner. We had encountered this erroneous attitude quite frequently in the last few months.

The wounded were soon settled for a rest, while the three of us went to work to remove the messes that covered the wounds. Some people had white paper bandages while some had used tooth powder to stop bleeding. It was amazingly effective. Our problem was to remove the caked stuff without causing any recurrence of bleeding.

Our trip back to Lanhsien was a fast one. We stayed ahead of the stretchers. Doctors Jong and Li periodically went up the line of stretchers to dispense painkillers or tea.

What a reception we received from headquarters' staff, including Ho Lung. We were guests of the commander for supper. During the meal we told him of our experiences. Later, half-jesting, he patted me on the head saying, "Well, *Yang kuie tse*, what will your people expect when the Imperial armies of Japan invade your country?" Here indeed was food for thought, especially for the white people who lived in the international settlements of China's big cities. Would they believe that because they were white the Japanese soldiers would treat them with mercy?

This life was beginning to show on me. I had lost so much weight that my uniform hung on me like a sack on a fence post. Vitamin deficiencies plagued me. I decided it was time to get going. I asked Ho Lung if I could have a pass back to Yenan.

"Oh sure! You are no good here anyway, always wanting something we haven't got!" he laughed. But he was sure that I would want to stay until Dr. Jong's wedding, which would be sometime around September fifth.

The girl had finally said yes. Dr. Jong came in for a most unmerciful ribbing. The chief of staff, Hsiao Ke, was a master of nuances and he asked questions with a double meaning to confuse people. He wanted to know if Dr. Jong's bride was a virgin! This was all he was interested in but he felt Dr. Jong was lucky; he knew what the girl looked like. He didn't have to wait till he removed the bride's veil to see if he had a beauty or a beast–he already had the beast! Eventually, Dr. Jong became angry with the question.

The big wedding was different from an ordinary Chinese wedding. There was no mother-in-law to be catered to. Ho Lung insisted that he was really the bride's father-in-law so he provided the banquet. The tables were decorated with gaudy paper flowers of gigantic size and a flower archway was built over the bride and groom. The bride's students presented her with many gifts: quilts, linens, pots and pans. I gave her a pair of white woollen blankets that I had been lugging around but had never used. I was glad to be rid of them. All the comrades wished the couple much happiness and many sons. They would reside at the medical centre in Dr. Jong's quarters. The bride continued teaching under her own name. She considered homemaking only a sideline.

On a bright sunny September morning I started to retrace my steps to Shensi. At four A.M., my *hsiao kiue* was excitedly jumping around, making tea, eating his own breakfast, and packing my belongings, books, and souvenirs. By the time the sun was well up, people came to say goodbye, to tell me how much they would miss me, and to thank me for whatever I had done for them. Although I could not see that I had done anything, I had learned a lot, and I had come to know Ho Lung, who was one of my favourite Red Army commanders. I decided to go and take leave of him, but before I knew it Ho was at my house talking about how glad he was that I had come to the 120th and how much they appreciated what I had done.

Once we were mounted on horses, Ho Lung and his men accompanied us out through the gates of Lanhsien. He said he wanted to make sure I didn't break down and come back, then with a laugh he turned and was gone.

I was riding one of those big Japanese horses and felt a little awkward. The head of the company was a tough-looking fellow and he wasn't going to stop till we got to Shui Teh.

My companion, a young woman teacher, Li Jen, who was going to Kong Tah for the first time, asked many questions about Yenan. At the end of two days we had crossed the

Yellow River and Li Jen and I were feeling the effects of the rough ride. This was by far the roughest trip I had ever made, with no time to rest. We had reserved a place on the China postal truck, sitting on top of the mail bags. Had we not had a breakdown we would have made Yenan the same night. We stayed at one of the small villages along the way and ate supper with the family—eggplant, red peppers, ginger, and noodles with hot bread and tea. We bedded down with the children.

We were on the way bright and early. As we neared the city of Yenan we were surprised to find the walls being demolished for defence purposes. The Japanese could not possibly hold a city without walls in this hilly country. The slabs of stone were to be used for roads.

Suddenly I felt like a stranger and surely I was. I no longer had even a place to stay, so I went up to see Dr. Mah. I found him at his cave playing cards with Li Teh and Wu Lian Ping.

We talked about Bethune. Old Li gave me a long lecture about being a quitter. He said he had known that Bethune didn't want me around, that he wanted to do things by himself and do them dramatically.

Around midnight I went off to find Dr. Jean Chiang at the hospital. She was surprised to see me at her door so late.

"Well, I couldn't get you on the telephone. No answer," I said jokingly.

"How did you know we had a phone?" she said. Wonders never cease!

I enquired about transportation to Sian. She said she had been waiting for nearly a month for a Red Cross truck to arrive, but the roads had been washed away in places due to heavy rains. I prepared to do some more waiting, but it didn't last as long as I had expected. Three days later the truck arrived and away we went.

My farewell to Dr. Mah was brief. He was sorry I was leaving but he could see I was not in good health.

As the truck moved out of Yenan for the last time, the hills were more parched and brown than I had ever seen them. Despite the bad roads, the truck pulled into Sian on the evening of the second day.

I went to the Eighth Route Army office to see Lin Pai Chen and Dr. Kiang. There I met another stalwart of the Communist Party, Li Hsiao Shih, a most extraordinary person, witty, cynical, and smooth.

Dr. Brown came in just about this time. He said they had quite a wretched time trying to cross the Japanese lines. His opinion of Dr. Bethune was not very high, but he said Bethune would get along all right because he practically ran the base. Everybody catered to him because he was also "party."

As we talked, Chu Teh came in to meet Dr. Brown. I did not remember him but he was quite insistent that he had met me before. He bade us sit down while he plied us with questions about the fronts we had come from. He said the Japanese were pouring troops and machines into China determined to bring surrender. Fighting had been fierce in south Shansi with very little reprieve.

Dr. Kiang was not surprised when I asked him for a pass. He suggested, however, that I wait a day or so to see how things were in Hankow. I would be in a fine spot if I got to Hankow only to find it had been occupied by the Japanese. He said there were almost continual air raids. A week went by. Hankow had still not fallen so I took the train to Chengchow. The Japanese occupied the area in and around Tungkuan, so they shelled all trains to and from Sian. However, except for a few shells that whistled over our train to bury themselves in the loess hills above us, the trip was uneventful. It was noon when we reached Chengchow, and a rickshaw took me, bag and baggage, over to the American mission compound.

CHAPTER TEN

The next day, October third, started off with early air raids; lots of falling bombs, which got the whole community out of their beds early. This continued through the entire morning. We could not see the planes because of the low cloud bank, but there was nothing to stop them. The whole sky was theirs. The sirens shrieked incessantly. At least at the front you did not have to put up with that noise.

A train was to leave for Sian at one in the afternoon and I decided to be on it. It was to be the last one out of the city. Rumours ran wild that the Kuomintang troops were going to blow up the Yellow River dikes to stop the Japanese from crossing the river. The next day that is exactly what they did, although the action was a little premature; the Japanese were quite a distance from the Yellow River.

At seven next morning I arrived in Sian in the pouring rain. A friend gave me money to book a flight on the Eurasia plane for Hankow October seventeenth. Time dragged, but when that day finally arrived the flight couldn't take off fast enough.

"You know that this may be our last trip to Hankow and you still want to go?" the pilot asked. "What if the Japanese attack us?"

"Impossible," said I; whereupon he showed me the bullet holes in the tail of the plane. Five Japanese planes had buzzed him not long ago.

"Not so funny, is it?" he laughed. "I was mighty scared, too, for a few minutes. I had sixteen passengers."

By five in the afternoon, the refuelling done, propellers whirring and everybody on board, the plane moved down the field. Soon it gathered speed and became airborne. I took a last look at the city of Sian. I felt nothing at leaving.

At seven-thirty the plane landed safely on the Hankow field. A bus took passengers to the depot where a policeman examined our baggage. In broken English he asked me what I was doing in Hankow. Where had I come from? Did I know that I was liable to be arrested? He studied my passport with great care.

I told him to come and see me at the Lutheran mission home at his convenience, whereupon I hailed a rickshaw and started for the home. What a different city from nine months before! Barbed wire entanglements were everywhere, and guards stood at the entrance of every concession. Now the burning question was how to find the people I needed to find, if they were still here. I hoped they hadn't been evacuated.

The next morning a lady by the name of Anna Wong appeared at my door. She had come to take me to the Eighth Route Army headquarters in the Japanese concession. Anna was not Chinese but a very blonde German lady. She was the wife of Wong Bing Nan, but I did not learn this till later. At headquarters, everybody was busy packing, getting ready to move to Chungking, for the Japanese were just outside the city. The Kuomintang had long since moved all of its officials to Chungking.

Later in the day, I visited the British Consulate to let them know I was there and to ask about transportation out of Hankow. They were sorry but there was nothing they could do about transportation. The consul suggested I stay in Hankow. The British Consulate would look out for me. He was a little astonished when I told him I would get out of the city before it fell even if I had to walk out. Little did I think I would be doing just that.

Comrade Chou En-lai suggested that I go on the Army boat with Anna and Wong Bing Nan and other Communist Party personnel. The boat was about to sail at a moment's notice, which was a relief.

Anna and I went shopping, but a few blocks down the

street we heard a siren and dashed into a doorway for shelter. A boy came out to tell us to move on. We took shelter in a lumberyard, hugging a stone wall for dear life to escape the shrapnel from the ack-ack guns. Nine pairs of silver wings kept escaping the anti-aircraft guns as the planes unloaded their bombs on civilians.

Hankow was a dying city but the troops downriver still held on stubbornly. Within an hour the raid was over. From the smoke it appeared that the Japanese must have hit something big. It was the fuel yards, east of town. In this raid it was said there were more than 800 civilian casualties.

When Anna and I got back to headquarters, a *hsiao kuie* informed us it was time to go. Everyone took his few belongings to the boat office. I had a small suitcase and my handbag: talk about travelling light. The ship was belching clouds of black smoke from her stack. It seemed to be held together by yards of wire. Cabins were just big enough to turn around in and the bunks were made of wood. Certainly they were not long enough for me. I couldn't stretch my legs.

The two commissars in charge were Li Hsiao Shih and Bien Jong Wu. They boarded shortly after us and brought the news that Canton had fallen. This indeed was a shock, for the crack troops of Kuomintang were fighting there. Both Li and Bien had come through the Long March and were well aware of what could happen. They gave orders to leave immediately, for the siege of the city would not be long and the agony would be quick. The Communist Party publication, *Sin Hwa Jih Pao*, was set up. A couple of printers stayed behind to finish printing.

The *Red Star* (as we named the ship) was loaded to the gunnels. Its upper decks hardly had walking space. There were more than a hundred people aboard: office workers, camera men, typesetters, a few soldiers, and guards. Anna and I were the only non-Chinese. On a barge tied to the back were crates of office supplies, desks, filing cabinets, office chairs, radio equipment, print shop supplies, and several large crates of medical supplies. As we struggled laboriously upstream we noticed the grey diplomats at anchor, peacefully ignoring the war. The sailors on board the *H.M.S. Sandpiper* and the

U.S.S. Luzon watched us through binoculars. We waved to them and they returned the waves most enthusiastically. The city of Hanyang was a mess, the charred skeletons of bombed-out buildings telling their own story. We looked through the glasses to see if we could see the Presbyterian hospital but we could not.

Two steamers went by in midstream so laden with people and baggage that the water nearly touched the portholes. A few miles out of Wuhan, one of the *hsiao kuies* poking around the boxes and barrels discovered two stowaways: a merchant and his twelve-year-old son. They pleaded with Li and Bien not to put them off the boat; they would gladly pay their way. Li and Bien went into conference and decided that the fare didn't matter much since none of us knew whether or not we would ever reach Changsha anyway, but the responsibility for their safety was their own.

The winds died down. The calm carried the rumbling echo of guns to our ears. About ten that night, supper was ready. Li admonished all to eat heartily for no one knew what daylight would bring. After dinner, all passengers and crew were assembled on deck. Li and Bien gave orders for the morning. The boat was to be tied up for the daylight hours, under trees if possible. Only three guards were to stay aboard as the danger of bombing was certain. Bien emphasized that nothing on the boat was worth risking any lives for. It was nearly midnight when all had retired. The swish of the water along the ship's side was like a gentle lullaby.

October twenty-first came in with a blast of a gong long before daybreak. As we left the boat for the day, Anna was accompanied by her husband. Bien, Li and I tagged along behind and two guards brought up the rear. Li carried the treasury, a small suitcase containing money belonging to the Communist Party. I left my purse aboard along with my camera and films. I was to regret this before the day was over.

I stayed close to Bien and Li for I was scared stiff of water buffalo, which wandered at will wherever their fancy or appetites took them. Li assured me that there was nothing to be afraid of.

"But Comrade Li, those hombres don't like the look of foreigners," I protested.

"So you are a foreigner. Well never mind, among all this native smell they will never be able to locate a *Yang kuie tse.*"

Comrades Mah and Chow, the two guards, went on ahead to see what could be obtained for breakfast. Comrade Mah said he did not especially like Hupeh, although he agreed that the girls were not bad looking. He was unable to understand their horrible dialect though. The peasant women were very hospitable and could not do enough for us. As cooks, however, they just didn't qualify.

The innkeeper's wife was a tall buxom woman who worked like a man in spite of her bound feet. She was very opinionated. Modern women were all mad, she said. What with bobbed hair and uniforms and big feet it was hard to tell male from female these days.

We spent a lazy day watching the farmers harvest the grain native to this part of the country and the last crops of millet, sugar cane, beets, and turnips. By late afternoon we all felt a little apprehensive, and anxious to return to the *Red Star* to start the upriver haul.

As we came in sight of the boat, I insisted that I could hear airplanes but the guards thought I was a little bit touched.

"After four the Japanese fliers get drunk for the rest of the day," they scoffed.

It was now near six. As we neared the gangway, a small *hsiao kuie* came screaming, "*Fie che, fie che*" (airplanes!)

Three planes came right for us as we ran for cover behind the dam. They circled once, the lead plane flying very low; so low, in fact, that as it went over us the vacuum it created seemed to suck the breath out of us. Just as it was directly overhead it dropped an incendiary bomb, which hit the boat midship.

Peeping over the edge of the dam I could see the boat in flames. Cries, screams, and moans of the injured and dying could be heard as the roar of motors faded a little, but the planes returned to drop a high explosive, which tore the boat's hull to pieces. So great was the force of the explosion that I could hear nothing for a few moments. The planes then made a wide circle, climbing to greater heights while we scrambled for better cover. One pilot went into a dive and for a fleeting moment he opened up his machine gun. I hugged my furrow a little tighter. The fighters strafed the village, river, junks, dogs, and even the poor old water buffalo and oxen. A single winger came around, and the gunner leaned out of the cockpit and threw grenades at objects on the ground. They must have unloaded a bushel of the damned things in the area. Three bullets sang past my ear and tore through my cap, which was lying on the ground. By this time I could hardly control myself. The impulse to get up and run or scream to relieve the fear was rapidly eroding my willpower.

At last they left for other targets. Out on the river a large Socony oil tanker had been hit and was on fire. Soon the whole river seemed like a raging flaming torrent, with great clouds of oily smoke towering skyward. About ten ships, including the big junks belonging to fishermen, were burning themselves out.

Suddenly I realized that my face and neck were wet. I touched my face and found it covered with blood and mud. My first thought was that I was wounded, but I soon discovered that my skin was still whole. I was sure I had a charmed life.

We collected our survivors but we could not find most of the people who had been with us. Scarcely thirty individuals were left and about ten of these were badly wounded and required stretchers. The boatman's family of nine was missing. He kept searching for his small sons, unwilling to believe that they were gone.

Under an elm tree a peasant woman hugged the lifeless body of her two-year-old daughter. Cradling the child's head in her arms she wailed tenderly, "*Ngai ngai*" (wake up). She kept kissing the limp fat little hand unable to realize just what had happened. Then she seemed to go berserk, screaming and beating the hard ground with her clenched fists. But there were no tears. After several attempts to take the dead little one from her, we left her alone.

The local gentry offered assistance. The medical service

unit stationed near the village came to the rescue. Their doctors dressed, bandaged, and cleaned the countless wounds of our people, examining them for bits of bone fragments or bullets. Patients in shock had no available treatment, except whiskey.

Comrade Mah was the hero as he saved Li's little suitcase with the money, which we would now have to use. As for the rest of our belongings, we had only what we stood up in. Li and Bien were more than a little overcome, not so much by the loss of the boat, but by the loss of people.

In spite of the ordeal the local peasants had gone through during the day they opened their doors to us in benevolent hospitality. "We are all comrades in trouble" was their attitude. Supper and wine were made ready for us at the *Pao Chang's* home. A *Pao Chang* is the sort of headman, mayor, or reeve of a rural area.

After eating we mapped out plans and a route to Changsha in Hunan. Li dispatched two of the fellows to Changsha for help and to let Eighth Route Army headquarters know what had happened.

There was no place to sleep but the damp ground of the floor, although our host loaned us a rough, padded cotton quilt to cover ourselves with. One quilt for five people! The combination of cotton clothes and a bitterly cold night made my shoulders and right leg ache. The ache bothered me so much I could not rest or sleep, so I got up and went out of doors, where I found a nice large straw pile which I climbed into, leaving nothing but my head out. Silence and peace crept softly over the earth. A million stars twinkled in the velvety black heavens.

I was nearly asleep when a voice called my name and a light flashed. Comrade Mah and Bein Jong Wu were looking for me. I was touched by their concern and realized now why the Eighth Route Army territories had no refugees. Their organization stemmed from personal participation, and here participation was certainly personal. I felt a kinship with these people that I had never felt before in my life. Was it our common danger and our common fate that made us depend on one another?

The men wanted to know if I was going to stay in the straw for the night. I said I was as it was the warmest place I could find. They bade me goodnight, saying that they would be back later to see if I were all right.

Morning revealed us a down-at-heels, weary outfit. The party broke up into groups of no more than six persons each. The idea was to keep going. The wounded were carried on improvised stretchers or sedan chairs. Our destination and meeting place was a small village called Hsia Ho.

A short hike through the marshlands along a narrow foot-path ended where two sampans were idly anchored to the bullrushes. Nearby in a small straw hut an old fisherman sat on a tiny bamboo stool smoking a long pipe. He pretended to be very busy paring his toenails. His face and hands did not seem to ever have had a close acquaintance with soap and water and he had an aroma of fish oil about him. Comrade Li spoke to him in the local dialect, dickering for a long time for a boat to take us closer to Changsha. A cigarette and a cup of tea came before the passing of cash. Soon we were speeding across the still waters.

At Hsia Ho, sampans were to be hired for the rest of the journey. Perhaps we could purchase a few much needed articles such as toothbrushes and paste, combs and brushes. Li and Mah went to find the headman of the village. When we arrived sometime later they had made arrangements for lunch. We were all hungry since we'd had only clear tea in the past twenty-four hours. But it was necessary for us to hurry to reach Changsha before it fell.

Soon it was time to go back to the sampans where we made the acquaintance of Lao Liu and Lao Tsi, the sixth and fourth sons of the house of Wong.

"Are you a Communist?" I asked number six.

"Oh yes, for as long as I can remember," he assured me.

Li kidded him about Communists being bandits and bad people. Bien wanted to know just what Li thought a Communist world would be like. Li said he didn't know, except that no one would be hungry. Number six bowed and added that he wasn't qualified to argue the point, but if he could at some time in his life see Chairman Mao he would have it all explained to him. He knew Ho Lung could also tell him, but Ho Lung had not been in this area for a very long time.

The Chinese, like other Asians, look to a man, not a party, for leadership. At the civil and federal government levels, the man is the symbol to be believed and trusted rather than the apparatus of state.

When the sampans were well out of the town, number six hoisted the sail. Fish and rice were our staple food for the next few days and I really enjoyed it. Sleeping accommodations for Anna and I on one sampan were very convenient except during the nights when it rained. Then water leaked through the mats that covered the compartments. It trickled down on the quilts, which were often sodden, and we could be nearly frozen by morning. The hot tea and rice porridge for breakfast helped alleviate the chill somewhat.

The inhabitants of this area were wretchedly poor. Number six told us that some of the farmers around had been taxed forty years in advance. They were so busy paying taxes they did not have money for anything else. Most could not even afford a single bean-oil lamp, but went to bed when the sun went down.

During the morning we got a call from the sampan carrying the wounded. One of the patients had developed a temperature and was quite delirious. Number six slowed down until we were at the side of the other craft. I hopped on while they kept going. The young typesetter, wounded in the leg, was in a most serious condition, with his wound oozing black fluid. We had nothing but soap and water and towels for bandages. I poked around the wound and soon located a piece of steel, but it took a great deal of manipulation, grunting, and cursing to remove the bomb fragment from the muscles with only my fingers and a chopstick. The wound bled freely, so freely that pressure had to be applied by tourniquet. The patient had to bear the pain for we had no sedation. At the next village all we could get were cheesecloth bandages and Tiger balm (an all-purpose salve) so the wound was packed with Tiger balm and gauze. I left the lad asleep and followed Li's flashlight through the darkness to the inn where Anna and the others were having rice and fish chowder for supper. Such luxuries we had that night—a basin of clean hot water and snowy white towels.

We were still in Hupeh. Number six boasted that that would be the case for a couple of days yet, for we had to cross a very large swamp. With favourable winds we would be at Hung Ko (on the Yangtze River) in two days.

The swamp land was now to be crossed, and it was bandit infested. Six more sampans joined our seven so we had quite a fleet to impress the pirates with. The togetherness was for protection. Comrade Mah sat on the fore of our craft like a watchdog with his gun across his knees. Anna and I were told to stay out of sight.

Time hung heavily on our hands so Li and the others regaled us with stories of the Long March. Some yarns sounded impossible, some were just incredible. Listening to their talk, I realized that they had never known any other life but hardship and fighting for survival. Not that the fighting was continuous, but there had been very few years when a Red Army man was not carrying arms.

When we arrived at Hung Ko the town officials had prepared a banquet and a place to stay the night; very nice, even if it was a precautionary measure on their part. Self-interest in China was often disguised as hospitality. We were quartered in the large attic of a teahouse with ladders as the only access. Two soldiers stood guard in the shop below to see that no one took the ladders away. The only favourable thing to be said for the attic was its dryness.

Before breakfast we took leave of number six and his brother. They had found a cousin to take us across the Kiang. The cousin and his two helpers were great hulking men with the strength of a team of horses. They towed us up the river for more than a mile before attempting to get into the deep water. Then the three big huskies worked and earned every cent it cost to put us on the south bank. They landed us on the very spot Li had asked for.

At the jetty we waited for the rest of the voyagers before we split up. Some headed back to Shensi; the rest of us, including the wounded, went to a place called Gung An. Li and Comrade Mah went ahead to find lodgings. Li, as commandant of our camp, insisted that we stay for a day and rest and get a little extra nourishment, for we did not know what was ahead of us.

We departed Gung An on a large junk after replenishing our private larders with peanuts, oranges, cookies, and candies bought from a peddler. With some tea, these made a fair breakfast.

The day soon turned out bright and sunny. With the sun came the Japanese planes. The boatman wanted to turn back but Mah and Li bullied him into continuing. A heavy fog set in over the land before sunset. To avoid collision with anything we crept along the shore line from one ghostly tree to another until we reached the next town.

Li went to find the *Pao Chang* of the town to ask for suitable lodgings. The bespectacled old man went into a tirade against Communists and then the Americans. We got the distinct feeling that we were not welcome in his city. However, at a horrendous price, we secured sleeping quarters above a restaurant. They were fine except for the bedbugs and cockroaches.

Next day, Anna and I looked up the missionaries to get some dressings for the wounded. There was nothing to be had at the Catholic mission but the Chinese priest said that the Finnish missionary union had a dispensary at the other side of the town and suggested we ask them–after all it was International Red Cross material they had on hand.

At the compound of the Finnish mission we found a trained nurse from Helsinki in charge of the dispensary. Her English was not good, but her Chinese was much better than ours. She gave us the dressings and invited us to dinner and, of all things, a steam bath–the first one I ever had in my life. Anna and I congratulated ourselves on a job well done.

When we got back to our miserable quarters, Bien Jong Wu had been missing for several hours and Li was a little worried. When Bien did return it was evident he had been to a book store. His treasures included a book on the paradoxes which I was more than a little interested in. Since I first had come to China my one ambition was to study the philosophers, but I was either too stupid or too unlearned in

Chinese. We continued our studies well into the night, Bien and Wong Bing Nan being most excellent teachers.

The next day we crossed the Tung Ting Lake and hoped to be in Ansin by nightfall. There was very little population. Tung Ting Lake is famous in Chinese folklore. Love songs and operas had been written with this beautiful teardrop lake as a background. Ancient temples and pagodas peeped over the heads of the giant trees that skirted the water's edge. The water in the lake was so clear one could see the fish swimming in the reeds and grasses.

With the darkness, a great golden moon presented itself. In front of us the two other sampans glided gracefully. We could see the city lights of Ansin not far away. When we landed Li insisted that we go to the hotel and all have dinner together, for the next day we would be going separate ways. Our journey had been a bit rough at times but, as for good friends everywhere, parting was not pleasant. We had overcome much, and in each of us, admiration was mixed with friendship.

I went to dress my patients' wounds and say goodbye, then continued to my own quarters, revelling in the luxury of a whole room to myself, with a door on it. It was good to be alone with the prospect of slipping between clean white sheets and clean warm blankets. My delight, however, was short-lived, for no sooner had I hit the sack than I was notified that an ambulance had arrived to take us to Changsha. We were to start immediately as the driver had to make two trips before daylight.

Most trucking was done at night to avoid bombing. This ambulance was one of the first of a fleet donated by the Chinese Hand Laundrymen's Association of New York City. With the chauffeur yelling, "Come on, come on," we were again on the road. An hour and a half later we were deposited bag and bundle on the river bank to find our own way across to the city of Changsha. It was pitch dark, with hundreds of people milling around trying to get across the river.

Comrade Mah and a pal made a grab for an empty scow. We had no oars but we occupied the barge while the ingenious Mah went off to look for some. He came back a little while later with the great paddles hoisted over his shoulder. None of us knew a thing about boats or rowing, especially in the dark. The river was treacherous, with a deep undercurrent. Three times we got caught in the current and went round and round like a merry-go-round while we were carried further downstream. We weren't far off the Changsha side when someone threw us a rope.

The small hours had already struck when we arrived at the Eighth Route Army headquarters in Changsha. It had been a long walk through the silent and deserted streets of the town. At three in the morning we were having tea and talking with Agnes Smedley, Chou En-lai, and Yeh Jen Ying. We received a most cordial welcome from Comrade Chou, which I felt was a little unusual, for this man didn't get excited about anything, much less a couple of ragamuffins.

"You!" he said to me. "How come you always manage to get lost?"

Temporary sleeping quarters were quickly arranged. Up three flights of rickety stairs we crawled to another attic with single rooms and trestle beds.

On Armistice Day, November eleventh, I went in search of the British Consul about a provisional passport to get me at least to Shanghai. A servant said the consul had just gone out.

"When will he be back?" I wanted to know.

"Maybe not come back at all," was his reply. After considerable argument I sent a note with a servant. I sat down, saying I would wait till the messenger returned.

An hour elapsed. The messenger returned with a note from Captain Eames, skipper of the *H.M.S. Sandpiper*. The gunboat's launch would pick me up at the jetty in half an hour. Chou En-lai's chauffeur drove us to the docks where the launch was waiting for me.

As I boarded, the two tars saluted me and helped me aboard. I must have been an odd-looking tramp in an Eighth Route Army blue uniform and straw sandals, my face brown and freckled, my hair straggly and stringy, and my nose beaming. How I wished that some fairy godmother might at that moment lift a magic wand to give me a perm, some lipstick, and at least a new uniform. When the launch reached the *Sandpiper's* side, I climbed the gangway to the deck where I was met by Captain Eames, tall, very handsome, and much too charming. He questioned me at length about myself, and what I had been doing in the northwest. In the midst of a sherry the bloody air siren went off. I could not leave till the all clear sounded nearly one hour later. Returning to the barracks, I was surprised to find Dr. R. K. S. Lim there in conference with Mr. Chou. He was very cordial, and volunteered any assistance I might need.

In the end it took Anna, Wong Bing Nan and I three days to reach Hengyang by truck and ferry. In Hengyang, we decided to try to make Kweilin, Kwangsi by train. We reached the station to find it piled high with baggage, and crowded with women and children and babies. After a few weeks of bombing, life here was pretty well disorganized, confused, and demoralized. A rather talkative fellow told us that Changsha had been burned to the last brick. We had left just in time. The overpatriotic element had taken things into their own hands and systematically burned the city down so that the Japanese could not occupy it. The Japanese armies, however, were many miles from Changsha.

Close to midnight the sleeping squatters on the station platform were awakened by a train whistle. Only a false alarm, a train from Canton. Tired and weary, we trudged back to Hengyang, past the ruins of bombed houses. At the hotel we found all the beds occupied so it was the floor again for us.

Late the next afternoon we managed to secure a lift on an Eighth Route Army truck. By early afternoon of the second day we were in the semi-modern city of Kweilin. Anna and I went to the Police Administration building in our quest for housing. They passed the buck to the Foreign Affairs department. A very young man escorted Anna and I to the American mission hospital. Miss Ford, an American missionary nurse, took us into her home, which was part of the huge mission complex. She offered us a warm bath and lunch. I don't think she ever realized how wonderful she was, or how much she did for me that day. Since we were both about the same size she very obligingly gave me one of her cotton dresses.

Anna and I then went over to the Eighth Route Army headquarters to talk with some of our friends. Chou En-lai had just arrived from a meeting. He looked very tired, but was cheerful and joked and had tea with us for an hour or so.

Mr. Chou said he understood that a car was leaving for Kwang Chowwan and Fort Bayard in Indo China next day. It turned out there was indeed a car going to French China but they only had room for one passenger. So it was here that I said goodbye to Anna and Wong Bing Nan. I have not seen them since.

My travelling companions were Mr. Lucas, an American official of De Fag who drove the Ford, Mr. Halperin, a freelance reporter for a Berlin newspaper; the British military attaché, Lt.-Col. Spear, whom I had met on the *Sandpiper* in Changsha, and Mr. Tao, one of the big shots of De Fag.

As we were getting into the car the air alert went. This did not stop Mr. Lucas who raced out of the city. We sped past the shelters, which had been blasted out of solid rock, out to where the trees grew tall, then he pulled up under one to have a look at the squadrons droning overhead. I counted forty bombers all heading in the direction of Kweilin and northwest.

At two in the morning, still tired, we again hit the road. At nine we spread a table cloth on the grass under a banana palm for breakfast. Rolls, salami, and warm beer were on the menu. While we were eating, a young man in a silk gown came along on a motorcycle. He stopped abruptly and ambled over to look at us from closer quarters. He must have been a rich man's son for he wore leather boots and a pith helmet. Spear asked him to have a beer with us, which he did. His father owned most of this land and he collected the rents, he told us.

We passed French Customs officials early in the afternoon of November 20, 1938, and went over the bridge to Fort Bayard, French Indo China. It was still siesta time; streets were deserted except for prisoners shackled together at the ankles, cleaning up papers or sweeping the streets. This was French colonialism. Guards carried rifles and cat-o'-nine-tails to see that no prisoners escaped or leaned on their shovels or brooms too long.

We made connections with a ship leaving that day for Hong Kong. There were several missionaries aboard from Chungking, plus squawling pigs, bawling sheep, hens, and crying babies, all making quite a racket together.

Next evening saw us in Hong Kong, one of the world's most exciting cities. Long before we heaved into harbour, the lights glittered and sparkled like a jewelled necklace. When we tied at anchor, a motor launch took us to the Kowloon side. We did not wish our friends in Hong Kong to see us in such a dishevelled state so we decided to go to a hotel–the Peninsula no less–one of the posher places.

The White Russian doorman opened the door for us but one could see he was not pleased. The night clerk looked down his snubby nose, too, demanding references and saying he did not know if there were any vacancies.

Spear handed him his card with the official British war crest on it and the walls of Jericho fell. The clerk bowed graciously, enquiring if the eighth floor would do.

Early next morning, I jumped out of my most luxurious bed in a hurry at the sound of airplane motors. It was only the China Clipper coming in from Manila. Life was very beautiful in the morning in this well-ordered colony. I picked up the telephone, ordered breakfast, and made an appointment with a hairdresser. I needed to find a dress shop, buy some silk stockings, and get on with being a female again.

When the new me emerged I went down to the Peninsula foyer. There Halperin and Spear were having an animated conversation about something. I went up to Spear, tapped him on the arm and asked him if he would like to buy me a drink.

He looked at me blankly and asked, "Do I know you?"

Then he suddenly realized who I was. "My God," he said, "I didn't know you!"

I was in Hong Kong about three or four days before I got passage on a Dutch steamer bound for Shanghai. At Amoy the Japanese quarantine officers came aboard with doctors to make sure we were inoculated before landing. This didn't affect me as I was not landing in Amoy. Forty-eight hours later the steamer ploughed up the Whangpoo River to the British concession jetty. I hardly knew what to expect, never having landed in an occupied zone. To make matters more interesting, Evans Carlson had been there a few days before, and there on the editorial page of the *Shanghai Times* was a photograph of me in Army uniform.

CHAPTER ELEVEN

I hadn't been in Shanghai long before I found myself once again asked to go on a mission. Dr. Sheng, the chief medical officer of the New Fourth Army, was a very persuasive man. I met him at the Cathay Hotel where we talked about Anhwei and the New Fourth Army's medical staff's needs. He explained that Agnes Smedley was there, and she had asked him to send supplies.

Later I was invited to meet the British ambassador, Sir Archibald Clark Kerr. He sent an embassy Rolls, complete with crest, flags, and a chauffeur to pick me up. Sir Archibald greeted me from behind a magnificent mahogany desk. He had also received a letter from Agnes Smedley asking him to give Dr. Sheng assistance in collecting medical and surgical supplies. Although he could not openly assist combatants of either side, he said that if I would take the supplies into Anhwei he would see what he could do for the area's civilian population.

"Would you like to go to Anhwei?" he asked.

"No," I assured him. "I would not."

He argued that it would only be for a few weeks, and that my help would be appreciated. "But," he went on, "I should tell you that if you do go and are captured by the Japanese, the British government could not give you any assistance."

Despite many misgivings, I finally agreed to help collect supplies and take them to Anhwei. It took many weeks, but eventually we had gathered together and crated all the clothes, medications, and blankets we could find. It was agreed that four people would accompany the shipment: Dr. Sheng, a newspaper man, a soldier, and me.

We sailed shortly after New Year's on an Italian ship whose captain made a small fortune on the run to Wenchou. The ship flew Mussolini's fascist flag and the Japanese navy never gave her any trouble.

From Wenchou we went up river to Chingtien, which we reached about suppertime. We ate in an open-air restaurant, where crowds gawked in astonishment at the way I handled chopsticks, making stupid remarks about my clothes and hair. As I was wearing trousers they weren't sure whether I was male or female. No one told them so they kept on guessing.

With Dr. Sheng and the newsman, I set out to find Father Desmond Stringer's mission. When we walked into the mission house (doors were never shut or locked) Father Stringer was playing the piano, with his back to the door. He remained unaware of our presence till he started to play "Song at Twilight" and I shattered his reverie with the lyrics. I sing like a meadowlark with chronic laryngitis. He turned around as if he had been shot.

"Well, I'll be!" he said. Father Stringer, a native of Vancouver Island, was tall and blond with almost too much charm and blarney to be a missionary. Some of his friends in Shanghai had given me some gifts for him, which he appreciated since mail and freight were most unreliable.

We accepted the gracious man's invitation to supper and spent a very enjoyable evening. The party broke up about eleven as Dr. Sheng insisted that we must get some rest.

In the meantime, trucks had come from Kinhwa to load all the cargo. Chu, the chauffeur, insisted that he would wake us at dawn, for he didn't want to be late getting to Kinhwa.

At five-thirty next morning, the first bells rang for early mass. After mass, we went for coffee in the mission house. When we took leave of Father Stringer, he gave us his blessings for a road of peace.

We stopped at a small village for lunch, and the afternoon was almost over when Chu took us through the ancient walls of the city of Kinhwa. Such a dirty, unkempt city I had not seen for a good while, but business seemed to be booming. Inns and hotels were filled to capacity, so it looked as though we might be sleeping on the truck. One of the *hsiao kuies* went off and soon returned to say he had found a place big enough for all.

The anticipated visit from the police occurred just as we were stowing our bundles. They scrutinized our military passes, which had been issued at Shanghai by the representatives of the Chinese partisan underground council. In nearly all the large occupied cities it was possible to contact the partisans if one knew where and how. They had even infiltrated the puppet governments. The local constabulary looked at our luggage and papers, asked innumerable questions and, seemingly satisfied, went away.

Half an hour later the governor's own guards came round to see us. News travels fast. They were sent by the governor, General Ku Djah Tung, because the honourable gentleman was the boss of the Third War Zone and we were in his territory. General Ku's anti-Communist frenzy gained him the reputation of slaughtering wives and children of Eighth Route Army soldiers. It was said that the governor could not stop the Communists from infiltrating his own army and administration, so he took his rage out on the wives and children. He was, nevertheless, a brave man.

His men asked an astounding number of questions, even asking where my parents were born and if they were married. When they had finished rummaging, the soldier in charge saluted us ceremoniously, saying, "We are very sorry, but we shall have to put a guard around the hotel so that you will have ample protection." Dr. Sheng felt that this protective custody was not unreasonable since all foreigners were not necessarily friends of China.

Next morning we were on the road at six. The guards escorted us to the city gates to make sure we were on our way. We were most thankful when we sighted the small town of Ansi on the Anhwei-Chekiang border. Soldiers and guards were most polite, asking a few particulars and then waving us across the barrier into the New Fourth Army district.

Trucks of soldiers passed through the town, heading for

Kinhwa. The road out of Ansi cut through paddy fields, not yet under cultivation but sodden with water and mulch. This road was not very long, and at Tai Ping the motorized journey came to an end. It was now a case of leg power.

At this small town there were many girl cadres from Kong Ta in Yenan and quite a number of fellows who had made the trip from Shansi with Dr. Bethune and myself. The town itself was deserted and necessities were a problem; no food, water, or fuel. Japanese planes had smashed the town a few days before, so the population had moved out. The grapevine, however, was very efficient. There had been a great number of casualties, and when word went out that a doctor and a nurse were present, the wounded were soon carried back. The minor injuries were looked after; the more seriously wounded we took with us to the rear base hospital.

Our sojourn in this little town did not last long. We had to make San Men as soon as possible and now we travelled through dense bamboo forests. Everything was made of bamboo–houses, boats, rafts, chairs, and stools.

In our host's domicile at Tan Men, great baskets of tea were standing in the courtyard, while inside the dark rooms, several women were picking over the tea by lantern light, grading it according to maturity and size of leaf. These women were all from the family of Mr. Wong, innkeeper, postmaster, plantation owner, and official letter writer for the village. I wondered how long it would take our girls from Yenan to upset this nest of exploitation. Mr. Wong was of the old school, which was fast dying out in most areas of China. He was nearly sixty years old and had a large family of four wives, each with three or four children.

Next day we spent rafting, not a sport but rather a mode of travel in these parts. The cheap bamboo rafts did not have superstructures of any kind and only boxes to sit on. But they glided smoothly with the current although one tended to get wet crossing rapids.

We arrived at the rear base hospital of the New Fourth Army in pouring rain when there was not a soul in sight. The hospital was situated on a small deep stream in a village that was the supply centre for all the Army units who were fighting up and down the Yangtze River. The staff room served as a reading room, study, and lecture hall; and it also substituted for a dressings centre, judging from the big carton of cellucotton pads. This Army Medical Service had the only X-ray, microscope, and the only laboratory operated by trained technicians in the south Anhwei area. It also possessed real doctors and nurses from hospitals in the large cities like Peking and Shanghai.

Going in search of a doctor, nurse, or even a *hsiao kuie*, I stepped out the back door into the out-patient clinic, which resembled an ordinary market except for the splints and bandages and crutches. There I found Dr. Twie who looked up from a very sick patient. He nodded but did not speak till he was finished with his work. The doctor spoke fluent English since he had trained at the Presbyterian mission hospital in Mukden, under a dour Scots doctor from Edinburgh.

Soon Agnes Smedley appeared with Chen Yi, one of the commanders, whom she introduced to me. I gave her the gift from the British ambassador, a bottle of fine Scotch. Agnes herself did not look much different from our last encounter more than a year ago in Hankow. Even though her hair was greyer, it still fell in an unruly peek-a-boo fashion over her left eye.

My first impression of Chen Yi was of one hostile individual. He seemed like a very arrogant young man who insisted on having his own way. Agnes said he was a rough diamond. I took her word for it. As head of the political department, which controlled the New Fourth Army, including hospitals and administration and most of the staff, he gave me the impression that the sun only rose in the mornings to hear or see Chen Yi.

At tea time, Dr. Chan, the only woman doctor, came in with the head nurse, Miss Yang. Dr. Chan was a tiny woman with a king-sized curiosity mixed with scintillating humour. Dr. Gung, another member of the staff, was chief surgeon and had wonderful hands.

Most hospitals were owned and operated by the church as were schools and universities. It seems to me, looking back, that the churches of the west had given China the incentive to be a great nation. One wonders how much chocolate cake and ice cream has been sold over the years at missionary societies' ladies' teas to pay for the training of medical personnel alone. Most of these doctors and nurses were not remotely interested in politics. They were dedicated men and women of science who came to the Eighth Route and New Fourth Armies to give of their skills. Many of these young medical people had come from schools outside China, mainly the United States, so that cultural, educational, and emotional ties with the west were long-standing and deep-rooted.

When the medical staff lacked equipment the nurses and doctors fashioned their own, using native materials wherever possible. At the potteries they made bedpans, urinals, washbasins, and toothbrush mugs for the hospital–all in one colour. The potters of Anhwei were at one time the Emperor's potters, so they were old hands at it.

The hospital wards and nurses' stations were in the massive stone ancestral temples of the landlord. Carpenters and tinsmiths constructed every conceivable kind of equipment for wards, laboratories, and operating rooms. Here we even had a caseroom. Wooden boxes capable of holding almost twenty pounds of dressings, tourniquets, and splints were made so that a dresser could be more efficient with the men in action at the front.

The out-patient department cared for some 200 patients daily. The clinic was divided into different divisions: E.N.T., surgery, medical, obstetrics, and pediatrics. Along with the patient's medication cards went propaganda cards.

The nurse in charge of the out-patient department, a Miss Tao, perhaps twenty-five years of age, was a fine nurse who knew her business. We were roommates during my stay at this rear base hospital. She took me around the hospital to her number-one interest and project, her classroom. Here, students were copying manuals for dressers and sanitation workers at the front. The translations for the books were done by the doctors, nurses, or teachers. All of them felt a responsibility to help enlighten their countrymen.

Miss Tao said they hoped to train quite a number of

nurses, male and female, but the people at the New Fourth discouraged the better-educated people from joining the medical units. Small boys, some less than thirteen years old, who could do nothing else but push a broom were sent to be nurses. Even an epileptic was a ward worker, with the idea that if he should have a seizure, what better place than a hospital to have it in.

As we made our way into a hut barely discernible against the trees, Dr. Twie joined us. There were beds down both side walls and down the centre. Wonder of wonders, the patients had real bedding, sheets, blankets, and pillows with cases–but we carried lighted kerosene lamps. On the end of each bed hung a chart. This was the only military hospital I saw with such a complete set of charts and records. There were thirty patients here recovering from all types of surgery. The young man in the bed closest to me had bandages over his eyes. According to the chart he was twenty years old, and had been blind from birth because of eyelids that did not separate. He was recovering from plastic surgery. For the first time in his short life he would be able to see the world around him. He was most intrigued to find out what kind of a wife his father had picked out for him; he had been married at fifteen.

A few steps from this hut was another, where the diet kitchen was situated with its great cauldrons of rice cooking. The dietician, a small, diminutive lass from Shanghai, never took her eyes off her charges. Both cooks and student dieticians made sure the proper food went on the right trays. They had some fifty-three special diets for diabetes, gall bladder, maternity, and surgical patients. The hospital had about 200 non-ambulatory patients. Diets were simple but as varied and as balanced as possible under the difficult war and crop conditions. Some kind friends in Shanghai had donated several hundred cases of orange juice, which had to be used for patients only.

A special bell sounded for the staff supper at the house where we had first assembled. Our supper was on the table when we arrived. The meals were invariably pleasant, with much laughter, jokes, and good humour. I do not remember seeing communication like this in any other part of China except the Eighth Route Army. Certainly almost all Chinese men and boys were male chauvinists!

After the meal, Dr. Sheng, Miss Yang, and Agnes escorted me to the quarters of the commanders where General Yeh Ting lived and worked. General Yeh had been a follower of Sun Yat-sen in the early days of the transition period from the monarchy to the republic before even the Kuomintang Party came into being. He had, in fact, been one of the founders of the Kuomintang. General Yeh had spent a number of years in the Soviet Union studying military tactics and had joined the Communist Party of China long after he returned to his homeland. He firmly believed China's only salvation to be the United Front of all Chinese. In 1927 when the first split came within the Kuomintang and they began their wholesale annihilation of Communists and dissenters, General Yeh had been one of the chief leaders of the revolt within the Nationalist Party opposing the government clique. After the fall of the Canton Commune in 1927, which he was a part of and supported, but with which he did not agree on all issues, he resigned from the Communist Party and went abroad. He had never rejoined the party. Steadfastly, he refused overtures by the Kuomintang and was hostile to its reactionary policy. When Japan invaded Manchuria in 1931 he returned to his China hoping to help weld a United Front. He failed dismally. The Nationalists fought Communists with renewed vigour. Only after the 1937 invasion of China by the Japanese Imperial Army was General Yeh again heard. His record was clear enough, yet nearly a year after the formation of the New Fourth Army men avoided his name. Here was a man acceptable to the Chiang establishment, but not acceptable to his troops.

Here at the New Fourth I learned that you could be a Communist and at the same time be hostile to the Soviet Union, which was the mecca of most Communists around the world.

During the evening the theatre group entertained us. A young man who had had a leg amputated below the knee by Dr. Bethune in Wutai got up and, to the accompaniment of clappers, recited a litany about how wonderful was Bai Chu en (Dr. Bethune). Dr. Bai was beginning to be a legend in his own time. (The next time I heard that recital was nearly forty years later when the Dung Feng came to Vancouver.)

We were staying at the rear base only to rest a day or so. We proceeded to division headquarters in Yen Ling shortly. The New Fourth Army units were always fanning out in different directions trying to get nearer the fighting front where the wounded could be cared for earlier. Doctors Gung and Chang accompanied us.

Yen Ling was a nondescript little town. The hospital was much the same as at the rear base except that it was in the large Chen family temple and was not as well equipped in either personnel or supplies. This was Agnes Smedley's home. She kept most of her books and manuscripts here.

After duty one day, Agnes took me to see Hsiang Ying, the Vice-Commander of the New Fourth. Like the rest of the staff who welcomed us, he was a Communist who had lived all his growing years in the movement, first as a cadre, and finally as a leader of the party. The only education or training he had was through experience gleaned while in the ranks of the party. In 1934 when the Red Army started the Long March in Kiangsi, Hsiang Ying was in command of the Red Guerrillas, as they were called then. Now he was well over fifty, of medium height, built like a pugilist with stony eyes and a quick smile. But the smile was deceptive. The revolutionary movement had made him into an austere, unbending personality who would adopt any method to attain what he wanted. He was credited with the character assassination of Yeh Ting. When we talked of foreign affairs he was most vocally hostile to the Soviet Union, and did not hesitate to express his opinions. But there was another side to this coin—Hsiang Ying had been credited with the training, co-ordination and organization of the New Fourth. This Army was reputed to be the most intellectually enlightened, effective force in the rear. Prior to the advent of the New Fourth Army, the Japanese had full sway in the lower Yangtze Valley. No one resisted, but with the New Fourth came bedlam. It was guerrilla warfare, where attacks were swift and occurred in a dozen places at once.

As we talked of the United Front, and of its beginnings at Sian, I began to understand some of the animosity and hostility that Hsiang Ying felt against the Soviet government.

It was close to midnight when we took our leave and returned to the hospital to find the doctors and nurses sitting around the table listening to a new radio. As we opened the door we were greeted by "This is London calling." The BBC, with a symphony whose music swept through the room like a wave, showered us all with nostalgia.

In the evenings we usually conducted staff meetings to discuss how and where to get the things we needed most to carry on with hospitalization and the training school. We needed a skeleton desperately. Some students refused to believe that there were two bones in the lower arm, or that there was only one set of intestines allotted to each human being. The idea that the kidneys filtered the blood was over their heads. Dr. Chang said the only way we were ever going to get a skeleton was to go out some dark night and dig one up.

The doctors, the head nurse, Agnes, and myself went as a delegation to see the commander about digging up a skeleton and obtaining permission to do autopsies, as a number of patients had died without any seeming cause. While the commander was very sympathetic to our difficulties, he was afraid that a serious situation might develop as a result of such radical actions, since most of the soldiers were from the local villages. The peasants were very backward and superstitious, and believed that a mutilated man could not enter the afterlife with his ancestors. They cut the noses off dead Japanese soldiers left on the battlefield in order that the enemy soul could not find the resting place of its body. However, the commander promised that they would have a Japanese corpse sent from the battlefield. The Army wouldn't care what we did with it. We pointed out that the Japanese usually carried away their own dead unless they were totally defeated, and that this promise, accordingly, could not be honoured. Dr. Bethune had done autopsies in Wutai so why couldn't we? I asked. Commander Yeh assured us that Dr. Bethune could not have done an autopsy except on a Japanese soldier. We said no more, but decided to go on a body-snatching venture of our own.

A few nights later a fog set in. After midnight we ventured out with spades, gunny sacks, and flashlights. The Chinese coffins were placed several feet from the surface of the earth with soil heaped around and on top of the box. Dr. Gung and I dug up eight graves, all of them infants. Dr. Chang and Miss Yang excavated five graves, though only one proved useful. The rest had been ruined by the soggy soil of the Yangtze. Dr. Chang carried the sack of bones back to one of the newer temples where there was an operating room.

A few days later when things quieted down at the hospital, Dr. Chang tiptoed around very mysteriously and asked me to come with her—she had something important to show me. She might have been displaying the crown jewels as she unveiled her pride and joy, a skeleton hanging from an intravenous pole. It was a nice job, all neatly wired, a monument of achievement.

Late one evening after a heavy day of newly arrived wounded, the litter bearers brought us a Japanese cadaver. With the bearers came a young male nurse from the third detachment whose eyes were wide with curiosity. He told Dr. Gung, with excitement, "We have orders to bring a dead Japanese soldier from the battlefield for scientific business. I came along also!"

The doctors sent several *hsiao kuie* out in different directions to summon all medical personnel, students, nurses, and dressers to this most important conclave. Before we knew it dozens of people were hurrying to the out-patient department, clad in gowns, caps, and masks, carrying notebooks and pencils. A makeshift amphitheatre was set up with stools and benches in a circle around the table on which the autopsy was to be done. Overhead hung a gas lamp, which gave a bright light. On a large table stood the empty specimen bottles. Doctors Chang and Gung were to do the post mortem, while Miss Yang and myself did the commentary, sometimes with the doctors' assistance. Dr. Gung looked very official in his long rubber apron.

He started off with a little speech: "All of us must realize that we are indeed fortunate to have such commanding officers who are most anxious to have all our students enlightened. They have allowed us the privilege of using this cadaver so that you might learn more easily some of the basic things about the human body. This is the first time such a medical procedure has taken place in any school in this part of China so far as we know. Certainly you are more privileged than I. When I studied medicine, our teacher's material was only plaster of Paris."

Dr. Chang, in her gleaming white apron and rubber gloves, proceeded with the exploration of the abdominal cavity and the alimentary tract. The students stood fascinated. There was not a sound except for the instructors' voices and pencils and notebooks at work. The man had been killed by a head wound. It was nearly midnight when Dr. Gung took the saw to do a resection of the skull. The scalp had been removed so that the bones of the head were exposed. Above the whine of the saw and through the partition came the familiar "This is London calling." The BBC played the Fifth Symphony with Sir John Beecham at the podium while Dr. Gung resected the brain.

After the autopsy all the specimens were labelled, numbered, and catalogued. Some drawings were made by a *hsiao kuie* and these, with material compiled from lectures and journals, would be made available to future students. It was nearly four in the morning when we retired. I don't know how the autopsy affected everybody else but for me it was like the first one I had seen in my training days. At my first autopsy, in an undertaker's parlour in Winnipeg, I just couldn't get over the old man's socks hanging neatly on the side of the coffin.

Soon there was another difficulty to trouble the heads of staff. No fields were being cultivated and the season was getting late, especially for rice. They called a meeting of all the farmers in the area to discuss it. A committee was elected under a commissar who drafted a line of action. In former years the tenant farmers were told how much rent they would pay to grow crops. Now this committee told the landlord just how much he would get. The peasants had no money to buy seed grains and what seed grains they had saved had been eaten to keep them alive. They now decided to plant crops that would give them a yield quickly like beans, corn, maize, turnips, carrots, cabbage, and melons. The committee went to the landlords' granary for seed. They paid the going price with some of the *cash* Dr. Sheng and I had acquired in Shanghai.

A co-op was also started to raise chickens for eggs and ducks for meat. Every four families were to have the use of a plough, harrow, and animals to work the land. It was the first time anything like this had happened in this part of the country. The peasants were a little suspicious at first but when the committee and the commissar worked out the amount of money or produce to be returned to the Army it went over pleasantly. The Army settled for produce. After all, the soldiers had to live, too, and it was easier to get grain on the spot than ship it in. Eating six months from now seemed to be guaranteed.

The politbureau now decided it was time to reorganize the area on a strictly political basis according to Yenan. They felt that there were so many new people coming into the area that this was necessary. The medical staff now had a commissar over them.

At medical staff meetings the commissar, whose name was Jong, explained why the Communist Party had found it necessary to politicize the medical and sanitation services. The New Fourth gave medical aid to soldiers and civilians alike. Outside of the Japanese-held cities, ours was the only help available. Some of the civilians and soldiers from other areas were hostile to the Communists and New Fourth but they accepted without question free services of the hospital, doctors, and anyone else.

A shocker came one morning when General Yeh Ting resigned. The Chinese government in Chungking, however, refused to accept his resignation or allow him to go to the Canton area.

Around this time the base was honoured by a flying visit from Chou En-lai on behalf of the Ministry of War, and also,

I imagine, for the Communist Party. Chou did not have the power to do much either way, for the political bureau decided the line the party would take. All he could do was restore a certain amount of harmony. He could do nothing about the tension in the medical services, except to say the service would stand or fall on its merit as a functioning part of the Army.

Chou En-lai had been at the base for nearly ten days when the politbureau met in a session. The medical staff was too busy to worry about sending a delegation. Agnes, however, gave us all the lowdown since she attended. The doctors and I congregated in her quarters to discuss matters, although we were somewhat guarded in our comments as her secretary and interpreter was always present. We were aware, however, that the medical section of the politbureau had continued their push to take over the hospitals, and that it was likely that we would be handed the old either/or bit.

Agnes decided we should have a little talk about my status in this situation. For this session we were alone, since we took a walk to avoid ears.

"I think you should stay for a while after the hospitals have been handed over to the Army," she advised, refusing to take no for an answer.

"I do not believe this takeover is the right thing, and I most vehemently object to mixing sutures with politics," I insisted.

I was wrong, she said. Since I neither had revolutionary tendencies nor understood Marx, I was hardly in an advantageous position, I informed her. A great many thoughts swirled around in my mind at that moment.

"I feel that you are making a mistake, that you will be leaving the Medical Service of the New Fourth under a cloud," she said with concern. Then she added, "I have been in correspondence with your father and I think he would not be pleased with your stand."

I refused to be hit over the head by my father's image. I reminded Agnes that I had come to the New Fourth to deliver some supplies and had stayed quite a long time already. It was on this note that our talk ended. We had been quite good friends and I was sorry she couldn't approve of me. In a few days she would be going to Chungking, and it was doubtful that I would ever see her again.

At five in the afternoon a meeting of all staff was called at which time some of the decisions of the politbureau were to be made known. At the start of the session the commander said he hoped we understood that this move was the best for survival. Anyone who could not honestly co-operate with the idea would be out of a job.

Actually, the recommendations were not so bad. The director of the new Medical Service would now have the commissar to deal with first. Our commissar was a good politician but he knew nothing about medicine. Young cadres were to work among the patients, teaching and propagandizing. The newcomers were to be instructed in hospital routine. I must say this for them, they went very slowly in the new undertaking, and I decided I could stay on.

It was, however, a difficult time to live through. The hospital was very active. Patients were being transferred to the rear base, while wounded from the front, which was only twenty-five *li* away, kept arriving. (A *li* is a third of a mile.) Hardly had some patients been transferred when twenty-two more stretchers from the front came in. It started to rain heavily and most of the stretchers and patients were sodden before they were put to bed, some wounded more than others. Behind the stretchers came a flock of ragged children who had come to the Army because they had no other place to go. Their parents or relatives were either dead or prisoners of the Japanese Army. The kids were first fed and then handed over to several teachers who took them to the school buildings. Miss Sung had a job collecting bedding, clothes, and other necessities for the youngsters. The kids apparently had a whale of a time in the bath house, a first for quite a few of them. The children soon became *hsiao kuies* and later cadres and eventually, perhaps, leaders of the Communist Party of China. They were educated by teachers who indoctrinated Marx into their lives.

The Party became their mother and father. They were fed and looked after, but the essential ingredient, love, was missing. Some of the future leaders of the Chinese Communist Party became unbending and rigid as a result. But they knew where they were going.

The filthy, sometimes lousy, blood-encrusted clothing of the wounded soldiers was either torn off or cut off, whichever way was easier. They were then given a bath, but not many of them appreciated the fact that the baths were given by female nurses.

A wounded Japanese officer had been among the stretcher patients. His anger at the partisans was great. He was contemptuous, arrogant, and anti-social to the point of frenzy. His anger exploded frequently but there was nothing he could do. "Brave men do not fight like that!" he would scream at anyone in sight.

But in spite of himself he got well. When he recovered enough to be up and around he came under the Enemy Work department, which screened all prisoners, keeping the younger ones, especially students. The others, officers and older men, were turned over to the headquarters of the Third War Zone in Kinhwa. Captives represented money, for the Japanese government paid handsomely for prisoners, especially officers. Sometimes the government reneged on the payment.

The prisoners who stayed taught Japanese to the troops and anyone else who wanted to learn. They also prepared propaganda for clandestine distribution in Japanese garrisons. The prisoners were allowed the freedom of the village, but they had a guard who accompanied them most of the time.

On March 5, 1939, the Japanese planes came down the valley, flattening every building and hut in the village except the operating room. Dr. Gung and Miss Wu were changing dressings in the big ward of the hospital, and Dr. Li and I were putting up a new traction apparatus when the first small-calibre bomb dropped not far outside the door. At the same moment, we heard a deafening crash and debris went flying in all directions.

"Trenches are over there!" Dr. Li pointed, shoving me ahead of him. As we dashed for shelter the Japanese planes circled back again, dropping a big black bomb with a deafening crash. The back walls of the temple caved in and our hospital was in shambles. Refined, level-headed Dr. Li was white as a sheet.

"What are you crying for?" he asked and shoved my head farther down as a strafing fighter missed its target.

Time seemed to stand still till the raid was over and the Japanese fighters headed off to the north. When I had left the hospital ward I was wearing a surgical gown, but when the raid was over I didn't have it on. I don't remember removing it or what happened to it.

The whole village was in a bloody mess. Six bed patients survived. Four attendants were missing. How many others were dead or dying, we didn't know. Out of nowhere I heard Agnes bullying her interpreter, Comrade Feng.

"Go and see if she is in that wreckage!" She seemed sure that we had all been killed. When Dr. Li and I emerged she heaved a sigh of relief. "Great Scott, am I glad to see you two!"

"Well, I guess we go to work for real now," suggested Dr. Li. Picking up pieces after an uncontested air raid is a very sad thing. The operating room was still intact as were the nurses' quarters although they were a horrible mess of debris and dust. The personnel at the New Fourth Army were fantastic people. Before we knew it, soldiers and *hsiao kuies* were clearing the mud huts that could be used. Most of the wounded were accommodated with improvised beds and borrowed bedding.

Midnight saw a very tired and weary Agnes tending wounded men, women, and children, offering water, hot tea, rice, or gruel to the needy. A *hsiao kuie* took us to the commander's quarters for supper, late to be sure, but more than welcome. That evening, Agnes slept on a table, her Japanese Army greatcoat for a coverlet, a bound book of medical journals for a pillow. With so much work on every side we were loath to go to bed.

"We will be working like mad for days to come," said Dr. Chang as she dropped her shoes on the floor.

At four in the morning the whole house was awakened by a very loud knocking on the front door of the out-patients department.

"*Shui yah?*" (Who is there?) demanded Dr. Chang.

"Open the door. We have wounded men here," replied a booming voice.

Dr. Chang gingerly opened the door and five men came in, four with wounds and the fifth carrying a small boy about eight years old, with a wound in his wrist so large that only part of the skin was left intact.

"Might as well get it over with," said Dr. Chang, trying to explain the boy's predicament to his father who only stared at her stupidly.

Dr. Gung operated on the boy because the father questioned Dr. Chang's ability as a doctor. Chauvinism! Most Chinese men were chauvinistic to a disgusting degree. At the Eighth and New Fourth women were given a status they never had before. We had women doctors, technicians, teachers, nurses, and heads of co-ops and no one ever called them anything but "Comrade."

One sunny day when things were quiet, Chou En-lai, Commander Yeh, Agnes, Dr. Chang, Dr. Sheng, and several nurses (me included) took off on horseback for the Third Detachment on the Yangtze Kiang. Except for the occasional buzz of Japanese planes, the languid tranquillity of the Yangtze area was undisturbed. Scenery piled up on every side. Far ahead of us to the left, great mountain peaks towered into the hazy blue sky. On the roads were thousands of refugees who had abandoned their homes and were now on the way to nowhere.

By tea time we entered a house where we found the Third Detachment. Comrade Yang, the chief here, was none too cordial to Dr. Sheng. The Third Detachment wanted six qualified doctors, at least thirty nurses, some hospital equipment, plus an X-ray–immediately. Yang was not pleased when Dr. Sheng replied that he would have to get in touch with the commissar.

"What's going on around here anyway?" Yang asked. "Why did the rest of us not have some say in the matter?"

After supper everybody went down to the Yangtze River dam to spend an hour or so gossiping. While we were sitting in the tall grass we heard a blast from a large boat in the distance. We concealed ourselves when a big Japanese cruiser

154

heaved into sight. On board Japanese sailors were drilling. The Japanese Navy patrolled the river twice daily looking for Chinese troop units. The battlewagon's guns were pointed shoreward as she glided by, downriver. The skipper scanned the shore with his field glasses, laughing and joking with another sailor while we were lying still.

When we returned to headquarters I was surprised to find brightly lit torches and soldiers singing and shouting slogans with abandon about the *Dung yang kuietses* (Japanese devils). But we heard an air alert and doused the torches. From the hills and the valley came the sound of falling bombs and the blast of cannons. The machine-gun chatter from several directions kept up most of the night.

In the morning Comrade Yang informed us that the largest New Fourth Army transport had crossed the river during the night. The gun fire was to keep the Japanese busy elsewhere and divert attention from the river.

After eating, we proceeded to the front clearing hospital, where a doctor, two nurses, and a dresser cared for the wounded. Supplies of dressings and instruments were very meagre, so meagre, in fact, that dressings and bandages had to be washed and resterilized so that they could be used again and again. Sometimes they could not get dressings ready on time and used white rice paper or moss from the hillsides instead. Patients were bedded on *kongs* in what had once been a rather posh summer home.

On our return to the Third Detachment, Comrade Yang said that the Japanese planes had been particularly busy all day. They had raided and nearly demolished a moderately large town not far away. We listened to the English-Japanese radio station in Nanking. They reported the fall of Madrid. I wondered if Dr. Bethune knew about it.

Agnes and Doctors Sheng and Chang were staying until there was an opportunity to cross the river and then they planned to proceed to Chungking and other work. Comrade Yang decided to go back to headquarters with us to badger the commissar for supplies.

As we neared what had been the thriving town of Nanling we were met in the ruins by soldiers of the 104th Division of the Fiftieth Army of the Central Government of China. They came to enquire, in a not too courteous manner, what our business was in this part of the country. Numerous cards were presented, then they departed, soon to be followed by another lot who came with an invitation from the county magistrate. The note pleaded with Comrade Yang to accept his very humble hospitality to dine. Yang graciously accepted, for where else could you get a free meal in this valley?

One of the *hsiao kuie* gleefully announced that there was a foreign missionary in this town. We went over to the mission compound, where we found a Spanish Jesuit, an old man who had been twenty-eight years in China and yet had failed to absorb any of the native people's tolerant, placid outlook. Here was a lost man who knew nothing of the world situation. He uttered a poignant "Deo Gratias" when I told him that we had heard on the Japanese radio of Franco's march into Madrid. His fervent ejaculation did not last long for he started a tirade against the Communists in China. He said he would rather see the Japanese destroy the whole village than have it occupied by the Communists. We left him still muttering along the street.

At eight in the evening, Comrade Wong summoned his entourage to the banquet scheduled for eight-thirty. On entering the *yamen*, or civic buildings, we walked through two lanes of armed soldiers. They were well dressed in woollen serge uniforms, by far the best dressed soldiers I had ever seen in China. The magistrate and local merchants rose to the occasion by dressing elaborately in heavy black satin brocaded gowns, the sleeves of which covered their hands by a couple of inches.

The fly in the soup came when the magistrate suggested that the troops of the New Fourth Army were lawless (perhaps because of their very tender age). Youth, to these oldsters, had no place in the order of things. Sparks flew from Yang's black eyes. He asked the soldiers if they thought they could make a better deal with the Japanese. Did their sons go away and fight or were they all safe at home looking after the good mayor's money and lands?

In the morning, the 104th Division escorted us safely out of town. We arrived back at the out-patients department in time for supper. I was tired, sunburned, and dirty. The operating room was going full tilt. An obstetrical patient was on the table. Dr. Gung and Dr. Twie delivered her of a huge child with no complications. There were many civilian casualties from the surrounding towns. With the extra work load the supplies were depleted overly fast so that now there was no ether, but plenty of chloroform. A young woman whose hand had to be amputated almost died when I administered the chloroform too quickly. Doctors Li and Gung exhausted themselves giving her artificial respiration; that and cardiac stimulants helped her survive to walk out of the hospital, though she wept bitterly at the sight of her bandaged stump. She had six children. Her greatest worry was who would make shoes for them.

A messenger came from Wuhu City on the Anhwei Kiansu border, which was occupied by the Japanese, with a letter for Agnes Smedley and a thousand Chinese dollars for refugee work. The boy was dispatched without delay to the Third Detachment where Agnes was busy with refugees.

Dr. Gung asked me if I would go on nights so that the nurse could go on holidays. During my interim on night duty Agnes came back to the base. She had got tired of waiting to cross the river. She had made plans for me to return to Shanghai where she had months of hard work lined up for me. In Shanghai I was to collect money and clothing for a project she had started for refugees. How I would get the stuff to her was something else again. We had run the blockade once but I doubted that it could be done again. Anyway, I was going home to Canada.

Agnes had not thought of two things while making all those plans for me: the progress of this war and the possible destruction of the New Fourth Army. The international situation might also bring war to the western world if, as Chou En-lai predicted correctly, Hitler marched on the countries of eastern Europe after the harvest was in.

The end of May marked a milestone for the New Fourth Army training centre. The new clan of cadres and trained guerrilla fighters were ready and the first class of thirty-five students was to be graduated from the Mini Kong Ta with nurse and dresser training. It was a big day for the whole headquarter's staff, since most of the top echelon of the Army was there. While they did not get along with each other most of the time, today they buried their differences and joined the festivities.

Everybody at the base proceeded to the athletic field after lunch. The big meeting was in progress when I arrived. Speeches, interminable speeches, were followed by the presentation of prizes and scholarships for continuing study.

Doctors Wu and Twie came to tell me that we were moving out early in the morning and they hoped I was ready to go, baggage and all. Any delay might strand us somewhere. The Japanese were more and more active along the coast. They wanted to make Wenchou before it was closed to traffic. The situation with the Third War Zone was very explosive and no one was quite sure what would happen. Whether the Kuomintang Armies would move against the New Fourth was anyone's guess.

After supper the doctors and I went to say goodbye to Agnes Smedley. We stayed till the wee small hours drinking tea, eating raw peanuts, and remembering the funny things that happened while we all worked together. During the evening General Yeh came in to say goodbye. Very gravely he thanked me for all I had done for his wounded and said he and his people would never forget me. I felt a little foolish for I didn't believe him.

CHAPTER TWELVE

Dawn had hardly cracked when we started out through the heavy wet bamboo forests. The heat was unbelievable. In the distance machine guns chattered endlessly. We rested during the heat of the day in the home of the quartermaster. Comrade Wong insisted that it was too hot to continue, and that we should stay the night. But we settled for a cup of tea.

By suppertime we were at the last hospital in the New Fourth area. I wanted to see the arsenal before we left the Army. I had heard that the Japanese and Americans supplied the guns and munitions for the Army. This enterprise was housed in a bamboo shelter. The men worked two shifts to produce bullets. Never having been in a munitions plant before I found it quite interesting. Barrels of gunpowder sat on platforms off the ground to keep dry. Some soldiers sat on homemade benches at a table filling large and small cartridges. Into the cannon shells they put all manner of things from nails to broken up pots.

We were on the road very early to make it over the mountains, and reached headquarters at suppertime.

Our chauffeur Chu had waited an extra day for us. Things were getting tough, he said, this would probably be his last trip to Chekiang. There was heavy fighting around Mingpo, and Wenchou was about to be blockaded.

We finally reached Chingtien and were soon gliding down midstream in broad daylight. We were on the river all night and in the morning tied up on the waterfront in Wenchou along with a couple of hundred other sampans.

I decided I would go over to the Canadian mission. There we would find out how to continue our journey. The Reverend Father told us that there was a boat, the *Jardine Matheson*, leaving almost immediately for Hong Kong. It would be the last one in or out of the port. We rushed to the pier, but when we got there the steamer had already cleared and was on her way.

The Japanese planes were over the city early. At first they did not drop any bombs, but went away, and came back circling the city. We were inside a restaurant having tea when the bombs finally came tumbling down on the waterfront. Somewhere nearby there was a thundering crash. Plaster broke from the ceiling, windows fell in, and the skylight crashed down. Lucky for us the shutters on the inside of the windows were intact so there was some protection from flying debris. We decided to return to Chingtien.

Once there, I went to see Father Stringer, who very kindly wired the British Consul in Fuchow for information. The mission had one of the three phones in the village. The consul replied that the *Li Sang* was in port and was to sail in forty-eight hours; sooner, if Fuchow was occupied.

Refugees were streaming into Chingtien from Wenchou, Mingpo, and other small ports. The mission compound was packed. Father Stringer had allowed his house to be taken over for the use of the children and the very old. Both of these groups seem to have the most distressing time during wars.

At Li Shui conditions were similar to what we had left, with refugees in all stages of distress. It was truly pitiful. There were no relief agencies at all. The civilians just took the crunch on the chin and smiled.

We found our way to the convent of the Grey Nuns of Pembroke, Ontario. Sister Angela had a dressing station in Li Shui. It had been three months since they had mail or money from home, and they were running out of supplies. We stayed the night, and after mass and breakfast in the early morning we were on the bus, bound for Fuchow.

Fuchow is an industrial centre. The harbour, on which the city is built, is a natural estuary–quite wide and with a very deep channel. Fuchow was filled with refugees, who received no help from anyone. The churches provided a bit of relief through soup kitchens and clothing depots but otherwise no one was seriously concerned about the plight of these poor people. Dr. Twei and Wu just shook their heads in dismay.

We hurriedly found the British Consulate where the consul extended his hospitality to us. He was most gracious, wanting to know all about conditions in the north. I asked him about the *Li Sang* and he replied that he had taken the liberty of arranging to get us aboard the boat. His chauffeur would take us there.

The *Li Sang* was a small coastal vessel. No one really knew when she would move out or if she would make it, since there had been almost continuous bombing going on.

Life in China those days was total confusion. Living beyond the present was useless but at least we were on British property. It seemed the whole city, including the river, was on fire—freighters in midstream were burning and junks of all sizes were aflame. It resembled a giant funeral pyre.

The skipper decided that it was time to get on our way or we might not make it. Because of incessant raids we did not move till well after dusk. The trip to Shanghai was uneventful. Once there, the first thing we did was head for our friends in Frenchtown. We were anxious about our people in Anhwei and our friends in Frenchtown were the only ones who would have news of them.

We learned that after we left Anhwei, Agnes and the hospitals had moved. The Kuomintang sent a punitive expedition against the New Fourth Army. General Yeh Ting was arrested and was later court-martialled and incarcerated in the house where the young marshal Chang Hsueh Liang was held.

Between the Kuomintang and the Japanese, the New Fourth Army was massacred. A few survived but any illusions anyone had about a United Front became a forgotten dream.

I left Shanghai on the last CPR boat out, the *Empress of Japan*. At tea time on the *Empress*, the passenger lists were set out at each person's place at the table. Looking over it, I noted in the first-class section none other than Dr. Richard Brown destined for Kobe, Japan. I could not believe my eyes. I saw him several times from the tourist deck. He gave me no sign of recognition and I wondered why. The answer came at Kobe where a crowd of bowing and scraping Japanese received him.

My welcome to Japan was somewhat different. Although I had no intention of going ashore a troop of Japanese police nearly knocked my door down. The two ladies who shared my cabin asked me if I wanted them to stay.

"Oh, please do," I begged. "If I get a belting or fall on one of their guns you will be able to tell my family what happened." The Japanese in Shanghai had murdered a couple of foreigners but the explanation was that the stupid foreigners had leaned on the soldiers' bayonets. The police asked me many questions over and over. How many men did the Eighth Route Army have? Was I ever in Anhwei? Did I think China would win the war? They left a guard outside the cabin till our ship sailed.

When they had gone, the elder of the two ladies said, "You must have been important in China to rate that kind of attention. What were you doing?"

"Oh, nothing," I replied. "I was with the Chinese Communists, that's all."

I arrived in Vancouver some time later. I was stone broke. As I watched the Vancouver shoreline grow closer, I heard a faint remembered voice saying, "You cannot live but one day at a time. In a few moments a whole way of life can change . . . you must learn to take one step at a time."

About the author

After the death of her mother when Jean was just eight, the family moved to Saskatchewan. Jean grew up in a political household — her father, active in the Communist Party in its early years, was one of eight party leaders sent to prison in 1931 on charges of sedition.

Jean graduated from nursing school during the Depression. Because jobs were few and far between, she accepted an offer from a Franciscan Order to work in a mission in poverty-stricken central China — even though she emphatically did not consider herself a missionary. In March 1933, at the age of 22, she embarked from Vancouver with two other nurses and spent the next four years in war-torn China. She returned to Canada in 1937.

A few months later, friends of her father's asked her to return to China, this time with Dr. Norman Bethune. Bethune had, by this time, already made a reputation for himself in the Spanish Civil War, and had secretly become a member of the Canadian Communist Party. Now the party was sending Bethune to join the famous Eighty Route Army of Mao Tse-tung and Chou En-lai.

Back in China a second time, Jean Ewen has a stormy working relationship with Bethune — in the midst of enormous hardships and constant dangers while they worked in Mao's army. As the Japanese invaders advanced, Jean managed to catch the last boat out in 1939 and returned to Vancouver.

In this memoir of these dramatic years, Jean Ewen offers a matter-of-fact account of what she saw and what she did as a nurse in China.

Other Canadian Lives you'll enjoy reading

Canadian Lives is a paperback reprint series which presents the best in Canadian biography chosen from the lists of Canada's many publishing houses. Here is a selection of titles in the series. Watch for more Canadian Lives every season, from Goodread Biographies. Ask for them at your local bookstore.

Something Hidden: A Biography of Wilder Penfield
Jefferson Lewis

The life story of a world-famous Canadian surgeon and scientist — written by his journalist grandson who has portrayed both the public and the private sides of Penfield's extraordinary life of achievement.

"One of the most valuable and fascinating biographies I have read in many years." — Hugh MacLennan

Canadian Lives 1   0-88780-101-3

Within the Barbed Wire Fence
Takeo Nakano

The moving story of a young Japanese man, torn from his family in 1942 and sent with hundreds of others to a labour camp in the B.C. interior.

"A poet's story of a man trapped by history and events far beyond his control." — *Canadian Press*

Canadian Lives 2   0-88780-102-1

The Patricks: Hockey's Royal Family
Eric Whitehead

A first-rate chronicle of the four-generation family of lively Irish-Canadians who have played a key role in the history of hockey for more than 70 years.

"A damn good story." — Jack Dulmage, *The Windsor Star*

Canadian Lives 3   0-88780-103-X

Hugh MacLennan: A Writer's Life
Elspeth Cameron

The prize-winning bestseller that chronicles the life of one of Canada's most successful novelists.

"This impressive biography does justice to the man and his work." — Margaret Laurence

Canadian Lives 4   0-88780-104-8

Canadian Nurse in China
Jean Ewen

The story of a remarkable young adventurer who went to war-torn China in the 1930s, met all the heroes of the Chinese Revolution, and survived the terrors and dangers she encountered with her ironic sense of humour intact.

"A remarkably candid book by a no-nonsense nurse."
— Pierre Berton

Canadian Lives 5   0-88780-105-6

An Arctic Man
Ernie Lyall

Sixty-five years in Canada's North — the story of a man who chose the Inuit way of life.

"The main reason I decided to do a book about my life in the north is that I finally got fed up with all the baloney in so many books written about the north." — Ernie Lyall, in the preface.

Canadian Lives 6   0-88780-106-4

Boys, Bombs and Brussels Sprouts
J. Douglas Harvey

One man's irreverent, racy, sometimes heart-breaking, account of flying for Canada with Bomber Command in the Second World War.

"Tells more about what it was like 'over there' than all of the military histories ever written." — *Canadian Press*

Canadian Lives 7   0-88780-107-2

Nathan Cohen: The Making of a Critic
Wayne Edmonstone

A giant of a man, a legend, Cohen had a vision of what Canadians could achieve in the arts and entertainment — and he convinced both audiences and artists that Canadian work should and could equal the world's best.

"A man of vision, prophecy and insight." — *Ottawa Revue*

Canadian Lives 8   0-88780-108-0

The Wheel of Things:
A Biography of L.M. Montgomery
Mollie Gillen

The remarkable double life of the woman who created Canada's best-loved heroine, Anne of Green Gables.

"A perceptive and sympathetic portrait of a complex personality." — Ottawa *Journal*

Canadian Lives 9   0-88780-109-9

Walter Gordon: A Political Memoir
Walter Gordon

The gentle, passionate patriot who became an Ottawa insider and fought for his principles in a cabinet of politicians all too ready to abandon theirs.

"Valuable insight into our political history and a revealing portrait of the man himself."

— CBC newsman Norman Depoe

Canadian Lives 10   0-88780-110-2

Troublemaker!
James Gray

The memoirs of a witty, warm-hearted, irreverent newspaperman who witnessed the golden age of Western Canada, 1935-1955.

"A book of great immediacy and appeal — wise and extraordinarily revealing about ourselves." — Jamie Portman, Southam News Services

Canadian Lives 11   0-88780-111-0

When I Was Young
Raymond Massey

One of Canada's most distinguished actors tells the story of his aristocratic youth as the offspring of the most Establishment family of Toronto. The first of his two-volume memoirs.

"An urbane, humour-inflected and sensitive recollection."
— *Victoria Times-Colonist*

Canadian Lives 12   0-88780-112-9

Having trouble finding a copy of a book in this series?

If you're having difficulty finding a copy of a book in Goodread Biographies' Canadian Lives series, send us a stamped, self-addressed envelope and we'll put you in touch with a bookstore that stocks all titles in the series.

Write to:

Goodread Biographies
333 - 1657 Barrington Street
Halifax, Nova Scotia
B3J 2A1

Be sure to enclose a stamped, self-addressed envelope with your letter.

g